MILES

FROM THE

SIDELINE

This book will touch your heart and your soul. I have had the utmost respect for Charlie and Maura Weis for many years, but it has grown since reading her book. It is easy to see why Charlie, Maura, and Hannah are loved by so many people.

Lou Holtz

There is so much talk these days about children with special needs. More and more families are affected and challenged and overwhelmed by their circumstances. Now Maura Weis tells her story so completely, so honestly, that you can't help but feel this is happening to you and yours. She can't cure the problem, but she sure can describe what the journey is like with a special needs daughter. It is so compelling you will feel every step of the struggle, but she will also explain the special joy and understanding of life that only these children can bring.

Regis Philbin

A story of love—of husband and children. Maura Weis beautifully recounts living life with Hannah, a child with special needs, and what it takes to hold her family together. This is a book of inspiration and a must-read for all parents of children with special needs, professionals, and especially those who enjoy a book written with compassion and a joy of living.

June Groden, Ph.D.
Director, The Groden Center

Miles from the Sideline is told with love and insight, giving voice to the experiences of families who share the joys and sorrows associated with having "special needs" children. Maura Weis's journey with Hannah also provides insights into a society that is struggling to accept and value diversity.

Thomas L. Whitman, Ph.D.
Professor of Psychology, University of Notre Dame
Author of *Autism and Its Development*

MILES

FROM THE

SIDELINE

A Mother's Journey *with her* Special Needs Daughter

MAURA WEIS

with JESSICA TROBAUGH TEMPLE

FOREWORD *by* CHARLIE WEIS

SORIN BOOKS Notre Dame, Indiana

All of the author's royalties will support the work of Hannah & Friends.

www.sorinbooks.com

ISBN-10 1-933495-03-0 ISBN-13 978-1-933495-03-3

Cover and text design by Katherine Robinson Coleman.

Printed and bound in the United States of America.

Library of Congress Cataloging-in-Publication Data

Weis, Maura.
    Miles from the sideline : a mother's journey with her special needs daughter/Maura Weis with Jessica Trobaugh Temple.
    p. cm.
    ISBN-13: 978-1-933495-03-3
    ISBN-10: 1-933495-03-0
    1. Parents of children with disabilities—United States. 2. Developmentally disabled children—United States. 3. Mother and child—United States. 4. Parenting—Religious aspects—Christianity. I. Temple, Jessica Trobaugh. II. Title.

    HQ759.913.W447 2008
    305.9'0840973—dc22

    2007046769

I AM DEDICATING MY BOOK TO MY FAMILY.

To my husband, Charlie, who is my soul mate. He has given me so much emotional support throughout our lives together. Because of his love, I have the confidence to meet any challenge that I face and have faced in this lifetime. He is a great dad and a great supporter of people with special needs, and that is not an easy thing to do as a football coach.

TO MY SON, CHARLIE, who always keeps me going and smiling. He has been with me through everything, and he has the heart of a champion.

TO HANNAH, whose love has always shone through since she was a baby. She has taught me that unconditional love is the reason we are here on earth. To truly love like this is the key to happiness. Thank you, Hannah, for giving me this gift.

TO ALL OF MY PETS, who are my therapists and who give me unconditional love every day.

CONTENTS

FOREWORD BY

CHARLIE WEIS

I T WAS THE SPRING OF 2003. AS WE SAT overlooking the ocean at our condo in South Carolina, Maura turned to me and spoke some important words. "You could have died, and we would never have done anything for anyone but ourselves." That was the truth. Parenting two children and coaching in the NFL didn't leave much time, especially when your daughter has severe global developmental delays caused, we now know, by a rare seizure disorder. Throw in an affectionate son deserving attention and me rehabbing from a surgery gone bad, and you could understand my selfish attitude.

Not Maura. People with "special needs" had become her passion. She was determined to bring awareness and compassion to any person with special needs. We were fortunate to make enough money so that Hannah could live the best life she could under the circumstances. Not true for many of those inflicted with an intellectual or a physical disability. With this reality at heart, Hannah & Friends was born.

Maura started this mom-and-pop charity with two goals in mind. To honor Hannah, she first wanted to raise funds to help those individuals with special needs who were from low-income families. To accomplish this, she began a program titled "Hannah's Helping Hands." While living the theme of awareness and compassion, she thought bigger. Her long-range plan was to build a residential community for adults with special needs that blended into a community in a farm setting with animals and at least thirty acres.

Fast-forward to May 15, 2007. The local city council approved the Hannah & Friends project to purchase and develop a thirty-acre plot of land in South Bend, Indiana, for this very community. In less than four years, what began as a personal lesson in life about being unselfish and helping people with special needs has turned into a mission to help people see just what individuals with special needs bring to all of us. Through her work, Maura has proved she is the one who is truly "special."

A coach's wife has a tough job. She takes care of the kids. She runs the house. She pays the bills. Maura does all this while never complaining. To think she could grow Hannah & Friends into a nationally recognized charity while dealing with the responsibilities of being the wife of the head football coach at Notre Dame is amazing. Since I met Maura in the spring of 1991, I have always worked ungodly hours. I arrive at work before 5 a.m. and often return home close to midnight. Our marriage works because Maura is independent and understanding. The responsibility of raising our kids rests on her shoulders. Maura has always been our family's soul. To have a loving marriage with good kids is solely to her credit. I am sure Charlie Jr. and Hannah would agree.

Miles from the Sideline is Maura's story. I am proud of her for all she does. Most importantly, I am proud that Maura has stepped up to raise awareness and compassion for those with special needs and has put herself out there on a very real and personal level. Most people in positions of celebrity hide behind problems like those we face with Hannah. Not Maura! Honey, you are the best!

Your loving husband,

CHARLIE

INTRODUCTION

S PRING CAME EARLY THAT YEAR ON LONG Island. I couldn't have been more ready for it that April day in 1997 as I cruised Northport's rolling hills. Everywhere I looked I saw green sprays of maple and oak, and all about blazed cherry blossoms and pink and yellow magnolias.

I beamed with the prospect of new paths, new beginnings. I had my son, Charlie Jr., four, and my daughter, Hannah, two. I had my wonderful husband and best friend, Charlie, who was enjoying a successful career as an NFL coach. We had just moved from Massachusetts, where Charlie had been with the New England Patriots as a wide receiver coach, to Long Island, where we would live as Charlie took over as offensive coordinator for the New York Jets. My husband gave himself fully to his job, and then some, and the teams he coached racked up their successes. But moving comes with the territory in professional football, and to go forward in the business often means picking up from one place and putting down somewhere else.

Our relocation to Long Island and the Jets just felt good. Charlie had been well received by the staff and the players. We lived in a nice community near the shore. My mother, who was doing well after a round of chemotherapy for ovarian cancer, had come to live with us, and I was enjoying her nearness. And the highlight: Hannah's glowing health report from her physician.

Driving the kids home from the doctor that April day, I was coasting on optimism. The news of Hannah's good health offered both relief and a reprieve from the concerns we had had about her since before her birth two years earlier. Now, like most "new" mothers, I could look hopefully toward my family's future. I was happy and grateful.

When I was seven months' pregnant with Hannah, doctors had diagnosed her with polycystic kidney disease. If she wasn't stillborn, they said, she would suffer kidney failure shortly after birth.

She might live twenty-four hours, a week at best, but her death, they warned us, was imminent. Though we had refused to believe the diagnosis— our gut feeling told us something different— opinions from several other doctors proved the same. Yet somewhere inside me, I had still heard, had still felt the presence of God telling me, "She will be okay." Doctors had suggested a late-term abortion. We refused.

I gave birth to my daughter, Hannah Margaret Weis, on April 7, 1995. She spent three days in the neonatal ICU, and then our black-haired, blue-eyed beauty came home with us. Doctors still expressed concern about her kidneys, though they couldn't agree on what her problems were or how to treat them. One doctor suggested letting time pass to see if Hannah would "grow into" her kidneys. Another physician suggested surgery to repair one kidney and remove the one that wasn't functioning.

Despite my reservations, Hannah had undergone the eight-hour surgery. She was two months old. After a week in the hospital, she was home again, this time with drainage tubes and an incision across the width of her belly. Through those toughest weeks, Charlie's mom, a retired nurse, helped us care for our daughter. And in time, Hannah was doing better; we all were.

Early into her second year, no one would have ever known by looking at Hannah that she had endured so much as an infant. Persistently cheerful and pleasant, she sought my arms continually. I loved it and indulged her. While she had crawled and walked a little later than other children her age, I made nothing of it. Most parenting manuals allow a generous range of ages for a baby's first steps, and I carried Hannah often. Besides, I reasoned, she had already lived through so much in her short life that her body and her brain needed time to catch up. More importantly, I thought, she was happy. She smiled and laughed easily, a mama's girl who loved both dress-up and sword fights with her brother.

But at her eighteen-month checkup, when Hannah received her measles, mumps, and rubella (MMR) vaccination, I mentioned her lack of speech to the doctor. He asked if she was meeting some other specific milestones for her age, which she was. And I explained that although Hannah could talk some, she used words rarely. I was told not to worry, that standards for infant speech are fairly broad. And I had heard that second children sometimes show a reluctance to speak, especially if they have a very verbal older sibling. Maybe all she needed was time.

Then came Hannah's two-year wellness visit, that joyous day in early spring 1997, when the doctor gave us the good news. Hannah was fine, he'd said. The view was rosy, and I had relished the moment driving home along the scenic waterfront. Our family was happy and healthy. Life, it seemed, was rolling along.

Soon after that tranquil moment, however, everything started coming loose. Over the next ten years, Hannah's developmental complications emerged, each one threatening to rock our family off course. This book is the account of what happened to Hannah—and to all of us.

First it was her speech. What little we had been hearing from Hannah at age two gradually faded away over the following months, and as her speech drifted off, so did our smiley girl. Concerned, I took Hannah to another pediatrician, who focused on her continually runny nose and connected her dazed state to seasonal allergies. The diagnosis made sense, so I accepted it.

Soon, though, the flares flew again. At parties with other children her age, Hannah was noticeably slower and unengaged. Toys didn't interest her much anymore, and she would become upset easily. I noticed that even a boy three months younger than Hannah seemed out in front of her, squealing at lights and pointing to objects and people. Hannah had never pointed.

When Hannah was two-and-a-half years old, we heard the word "autism" for the first time, and the world came crashing in on us. At that time, I knew little about autism, a brain disorder that affects a person's ability to communicate with and relate to others. But I did know that it had no cure. I was devastated. Hannah's diagnosis seemed like the beginning of the end to me. I was sure I would lose my little girl forever.

Not much later, we discovered that Hannah had a hearing impairment. She was fitted with tubes—twice—and underwent surgery to remove her adenoids and tonsils.

And so started the succession of therapists and evaluations, special schools and short buses.

Eventually, therapists and doctors categorized Hannah as having a type of PDD, or pervasive developmental disorder, a generic term used to sum up a spectrum of disorders (among them autism) that include delays in speech, motor development, and social skills. When Han was eight, we heard "mental retardation" used to describe her condition, and we discovered that she was having seizures. At eleven, Hannah's x-ray showed scoliosis.

To this day, Hannah, now twelve, can't dress herself or make her own breakfast. She has a limited vocabulary and feels frustrated when she can't communicate with those around her.

We sifted through seemingly endless possibilities, searching for Hannah's true condition and its cause, a process that at times frustrated me. For a while, we blamed the mercury in the MMR shot. (Among parents who've watched their children change virtually overnight after receiving the shot, it's a common theory.) But in our case, a blood metal test showed no mercury in Hannah's system. Later I suspected that the lengthy kidney surgery had triggered her seizures, which we didn't recognize for several years. Undiagnosed and untreated, some types of seizures destroy whole areas of the brain, leading to mental disabilities. Then at times I speculated that Hannah had a genetic disorder that science had yet to discover. We weren't sure we would ever have our answer, but we made peace with that possibility. Then, in 2007, just out of the blue, an answer fell into our laps. But along with this next explanation, we discovered that at some point in our family's journey, the reasons why had ceased to matter.

Despite her limitations, Hannah is healthy and cheerful. Though she resists our hugs, she finds ways to express her love and affection. And after a long hiatus, she's once again mama's girl.

Our hope for Hannah is every parent's hope for their children: happiness. Charlie and I know we can't *make* our daughter happy. We can, however, create a home life that will help her flourish, preserve her dignity, provide her comfort, and even foster her independence. In return, Hannah reminds us of our life's abundance. She has given us new lenses to see the true gifts of people with special needs.

With our daughter as our inspiration, Charlie, now the head football coach for the University of Notre Dame, and I started Hannah & Friends in 2003. The not-for-profit foundation focuses on providing a better quality of life for children and adults with special needs. A portion of the funds we receive goes toward grants for South Bend-area families who have children with disabilities. All other money is earmarked for the construction and the operation of a farm for individuals with special needs. Slated to be built on a thirty-acre property in South Bend, the farm will offer housing units, a common meeting space, a petting zoo, a riding program, and jobs for the farm's residents.

The broader goal of the foundation, however, is to promote awareness of and compassion for people with disabilities. And in this effort, our website, www.hannahandfriends.org, has proved a useful tool. It's there—in chat rooms at the site—that parents, caregivers, and friends ask questions, exchange ideas, seek help, and offer support and advice. There, they share their stories.

This book is also just that—one story, our story. It is the fruit of countless e-mail exchanges with other sleepless parents, of tearful and jubilant conversations with complete strangers after charitable benefits, of abbreviated phone calls with friends who experience the same struggles, the same "Ah-ha!" moments that we do.

Miles from the Sideline is less a chronological account of our life with Hannah than it is an exploration of our family's emotional and spiritual journey together. As with any quest, there are fits and starts, summits and valleys. In each chapter I try to explore a theme, a lesson learned. As we discovered, the messages are often clearest in hindsight.

On these pages, I attempt to portray honestly the challenges of raising a child with special needs and how our family tries to meet those challenges. I also explore some of the emotional and mental stages we have experienced post-diagnosis. Most significantly, though, I hope to illuminate the soul of the individual with special needs and the many treasures housed there.

For everyone raising a child with special needs, I hope this book will prepare, preserve, and encourage you. May it also help bridge those divides, sometimes within families, that often emerge out of insensitivity and misunderstanding. Finally, may it remind us all to open our hearts and minds to love's possibilities.

I do not regret that day in early spring so many years ago when I thought all was well. I do not feel foolish for my rush of optimism or cheated out of my moment of exuberance. I am that same mother, riding the same road. I still look eagerly ahead with wonder and expectation.

SHADOWED

BY

POSSIBILITY

H ANNAH HAS A CRUSH HOLD ON BARNEY'S LEG.

Here it is, her second birthday party, and my daughter stands cement footed, clutching our star guest, a purple dinosaur.

My son, Charlie, has just turned four, so this is his party too, and we've invited his friends from preschool. Everywhere kids bound through the house, yelling, laughing, taking each other out with couch cushions and throw pillows. Restoring order only when it's really necessary, the adults chat and buzz about; everyone is comfortable and happy. Everyone except Hannah.

In the midst of all the bustle, all the festivity, she seems seized. Locked down. Like a kid staying put on home base or stuck in a game of freeze tag. But Hannah isn't playing a game. She's not playing at all, not with the other kids, not with her new toys, not even with the TV and the VCR.

And not with Barney either. She simply clings to him as if her life depends on it.

When she finally lets loose, Hannah turns her unshakable embrace on me.

It occurs to me that maybe she's experiencing sensory overload. After all, pretty much everything in the world is "new" for a two-year-old. Maybe the party is too much, too fast.

Yet Hannah had played with other children who came to our house when we lived in Massachusetts. What is this?

Then it hits me: no kids. Since we moved into our new home in Northport, Hannah's big brother and I have been her only playmates. In our new neighborhood, she has no friends.

Yes, that's it, that's the problem. I guess I can't justify keeping her all to myself anymore. Hannah obviously needs more exposure, more social interaction with children her own age.

She'll start preschool early, I decide. It isn't my preference, but I want what's best for my little girl. And, just maybe, it's time I loosen my grip a little too.

ৎৣ৹

A few weeks after the party, Hannah goes in for her two-year checkup, where her pediatrician delivers the "all clear." I take the good news and run with it. But over the next weeks, concerns keep cropping up. Han still doesn't speak much; in fact, she seems to speak less. She shows trouble understanding me and isn't meeting the milestone accomplishments I see other kids making. She doesn't use her hands, except to clap a lot. And she isn't at all interested in mimicking what I do. I thought this was supposed to be the "me too" age. Instead, it seems as if Hannah couldn't care less about me, about anybody.

Every parent receives the same cautionary advice: don't compare your children to others, because every child is different. But Han's not just different from her brother or other kids. The most glaring difference, Charlie and I agree, exists between the Han we know now and the Han of just five or six months ago. Wasn't it our little Hannah who had set the table with her play dishes for Christmas dinner? It was. So who is this new child, so disinterested and apart from it all? Why is she so quiet? And why are we always finding her in front of the TV, eyes fixed on a Barney video, which she now prefers watching in fast-forward or rewind?

᎗᎗

Something is wrong.

Not just sort of wrong, but really wrong. On Hannah's first day of preschool, I feel more than the typical parental apprehension, more than that pang of grief that comes with "liftoff." This is nothing like what I experienced with Charlie. I'm a nervous wreck.

I'm a little anxious when I drop her off. She's not even two-and-a-half, after all. Until this point, she'd been with me practically every minute of every day, so of course I'm anxious. And as the day moves along, I imagine what she is doing moment to moment. Then the uneasiness takes over. Mothers will talk of a sensation, an intuition, an inner voice that tells them their child is in trouble. Hannah and I had always shared a tight bond, and I'd heard that voice before. There is no doubt in my mind that I am hearing it now.

I let a few more minutes pass; no call from the school. Hannah's session wouldn't end until 1 p.m., but by noon I am in the car. Hannah has been away only a few hours, but I can hardly stand it anymore. A warning bell goes off inside me; I have to get my girl.

I'm the first mom to arrive at school—a good twenty minutes early—and I discover that Hannah's teachers have been waiting for me.

As I approach them, I see their hands lying like a lace shawl on my daughter's shoulders, they steer her toward the door and bring her out to me.

"Is Hannah deaf?" one of the teachers asks pointedly.

I'm stunned silent for a moment. Then, as if someone has flipped a switch, I'm upset, angry. Do they really believe I would bring my daughter to her first day of school and just dump her, knowing she can't hear? What sort of mother do they think I am? I'm insulted, offended.

But they go on to tell me that Hannah wouldn't respond during class. And talking to her one-on-one didn't help either. "It's as if she's in a world of her own," they tell me.

I explain that Hannah had just visited her doctor and that we were told everything was okay.

Their reply: Hannah may remain in the class for now, but she'll have to be tested. Within the week, the state will be in to evaluate my daughter.

❧

Worry torments me throughout the week.

What will the evaluators find? What will this mean for Hannah? For our family and our life together? It's all I think about.

For one long, agonizing week, everything Hannah does or doesn't do, every odd or even not-so-odd behavior, sends a shiver of fear through me. Yet I watch her continually, unable to do anything else. She's my baby. So whatever the signs of trouble might be, I look for them, even though I am afraid to see.

These days are endlessly dark, deep. And yet we still don't know what's going on with Hannah; we have no diagnosis, nothing concrete.

But somewhere inside me, I do know. I have known all along.

It simply would take someone else's eyes to help me recognize what was in front of me. It's not just Charlie and I who notice Hannah's differences anymore. Now others, who don't even know her, see them too. And suddenly the differences are real.

This, I suppose, is what is meant by living in denial. For us, the specter of trouble had always been just that, a fleeting sensation, a brief and blurry notion. Then, ever so faintly, the light finds its way in. Dim though it is, that's all it takes. Now here Charlie and I stand with possibility looming large. No, we don't know what's wrong with Hannah yet, just that *something* is. And that is enough.

The bottom drops out from under me, and I am helpless.

❧

A therapist rattles a tambourine next to my daughter's ear. Nothing. No recognition from Hannah at all. Then she bangs a drum; still nothing. Hannah doesn't play it herself either. Not standard behavior for a two-year-old. Her heavy breathing concerns them too. My first step, they suggest: take Hannah to an ear, nose, and throat specialist for a hearing test.

That I can do. Their suggestion actually comes as a relief to me. Could it really be her hearing, as her teachers first suspected? In fact, despite the concerns I'd brought up with several doctors, not one had tested Hannah for a hearing loss, or even suggested it. Maybe hearing loss really is the problem.

As it turns out, Han has "glue ear," a painless condition in which sticky fluids collect behind the ear. For Han, this condition caused a 30–40 percent hearing loss in both ears. A significant loss, I'm told, one that could certainly account for her delayed speech. As fall settles in, Hannah is fitted for tubes and undergoes surgery to remove her tonsils and adenoids. As we expect, she comes through it like a trooper. The doctors are optimistic, and so are we. We should see a changed Hannah, Charlie and I believe.

Within a month of her latest surgery, I find Hannah sitting alone on the couch, holding a cup to her ear. She shakes it, shakes it again. Then a brilliance washes over her face. For the first time in her life, my daughter hears the sound of ice.

I'm overcome with joy, with gratitude. At last, we have our answer! No more digging, no more doctors. Hannah went into her fog because she couldn't hear us. This I can handle. She will come back to us, I'm certain; it will just take some time.

With the intent of helping Hannah's progress, we research some early-intervention schools on Long Island. There are three, and the state early-intervention agency insists I visit all of them. At one, an all-day school geared mainly to autistic children, I'm shocked by what I find. The school uses the applied behavior analysis program, which basically stresses learning through repetition and reward. The idea behind the program—which has been used with good results by many—seems okay, I decide, but the school uses food to reinforce right behaviors. It looks to me like people training dogs. What's worse, I see teachers putting vinegar on children's tongues to get them to say "no."

Before leaving, I meet one of the school's pupils, an adorable five-year-old girl with autism. "Hi," she greets me, and we chat for a few moments. Then, as I'm leaving, she says, "Hi," again. My heart sinks. Often, my guide explains, children with autism can't differentiate between meeting and parting. Driving away, I have no trouble saying goodbye to the place. My Han will never go there. I don't want her in school all day, and besides, it's not the place for her. All she needs is a nice nursery school, I think, and a little time to catch up.

∽

In the meantime, while she is being evaluated, we have kept Hannah at her original school. Her teacher there asks us to meet her at Chuck E. Cheese's for lunch. A friendly gesture, but one with a purpose, I discover. As the teacher puts it, she needs to see "what Hannah is like outside of the classroom." She watches as Hannah flounders around in the ball pit.

Now I'm really uncomfortable. Why are we doing this? The teacher watches my daughter's every move, studying her like an object under glass. "Sometimes," she says finally, "I think yes, Hannah is definitely autistic, and sometimes I think no way."

A shock wave of panic floods my body. Suddenly I have trouble hearing, breathing. And I can't think. What did she say? Autistic? In my head a resounding "no" echoes. Then I hear my own voice, "No, no way," and I'm snapped back into my nightmare moment.

∽

"Han's not autistic!" I keep telling myself on the drive home from lunch. "She can't be. She's my girl, and I know her." I'm furious with Han's teacher for even bringing up such a subject. Hadn't we settled this whole thing? Hannah had a hearing impairment. We fixed it. It's been only a few weeks. Can't they cut my daughter some slack?

But I already know that the issue won't go away on its own. A few days later, I call for an appointment with a neurologist, as Hannah's teacher suggested. There's a cancellation, and the doctor can get us in at 4 p.m. Fine. Maybe this will put an end to all this talk. We make the appointment.

I expect to have a good hour or more with the doctor, but when we show up, the waiting room is packed. I know from experience that Hannah won't last. I can't make her wait—not this long—she just won't tolerate it. But if we leave, who knows when we'll get in again? Against my better judgment, we stay.

At 5:30, when the doctor gets around to examining Hannah, she's having a screaming fit. Despite my and the doctor's efforts to make her more comfortable, Hannah won't settle down. She refuses to make eye contact with the doctor and instead stares at her closed hand for most of the visit.

From this, the neurologist issues her diagnosis. "Pervasive developmental disorder. Not otherwise specified, that is what your daughter has," the doctor tells me. A stabbing pain grips my chest. I look at my little girl. "What does that mean?" I ask the doctor. "How did this happen?"

The doctor offers me some explanation, though I don't fully understand it. Something about Hannah's condition falling within the spectrum of autism. But all I keep hearing is "autism." I leave in shock, with more questions than answers.

Driving home, I'm seized with terror. They're not right, I try convincing myself. Hannah just needs to get used to hearing again. The doctor's diagnosis can't be accurate, I reason. Hannah was hysterical in that exam room. It wasn't Hannah's fault. What did that doctor expect, making us wait so long? She couldn't have gotten it right. Hannah just can't be . . . The PDD label is just a tag. Just a tag they use to make sure she gets the services she needs.

But the terror never leaves me, because the truth is undeniable. Hannah sits right behind me, strapped snugly into her car seat, riding along on the way home to break the news to Daddy.

During Hannah's exam, I had requested that she receive an MRI in order to rule out my fears that someone, at some time, had dropped Hannah on her head. To our relief, the test shows normal brain activity. And within a few days, we enroll Hannah in the school for children with autism, where I swore she would never go. But still, Charlie and I aren't completely convinced of the neurologist's findings. It seems to us too easy to sweep her into such a broad category of disability, especially after the doctor had spent so little time with her. But we're being whisked through the system nonetheless. If Hannah's new school isn't right for her, we're told, we'll find out soon enough.

The professionals' approach seems almost cavalier. This is my daughter we are talking about, a special human being, a precious life. And we have to make her life right.

Night after night, I can't sleep. Hannah has started getting up at all hours, and she's impossible to put back down. On the nights she crashes and stays in bed, I wake up at 2 a.m. anyway and stay up, crying for hours. My poor little girl, what are we going to do? How did this happen? Why her? Hasn't she endured enough? And what will she become? The thoughts spool through my mind; I'm incapable of turning them off. I'm so afraid for her.

Every morning she cries as she leaves on the bus. Not even three years old, and my baby takes a bus to school. I've been told by school administrators that it's best for her to take the bus at least one way to or from school in order to learn independence. And shouldn't I believe them? But I can't stand to hear her crying. It's worse when I come to pick her up. I find her screaming uncontrollably. This is killing me.

I can't put her through this anymore. There has to be something else, something better.

⁓

And so were we ushered into the unfamiliar world of special needs parenting.

Eventually, we pulled Hannah from her school and moved from Long Island to New Jersey, which offered a broader selection of early-intervention schools and where we hoped to find more support. Charlie had grown up in Jersey, and I had moved there from New York when I was twenty-three. I had met Charlie there when he was the running backs coach with the New York Giants, and it still felt like "our" place. Our new home also had room for a barn where we could keep horses, one of my passions. Both Charlie and I, but most importantly Hannah, would be more comfortable there. We had reached the point where we didn't really care how quickly Hannah caught up but only that she wasn't miserable throughout the process. We found a more suitable preschool, where the children had varying types and degrees of special needs.

I did what I had to do and kept the wheels turning. But my grief was still fresh. My mind churned away for hours at night, and I always ran through the same questions, carrying on the same conversation with myself and with God. I spent more time than I should have trying to figure out *how* this had happened to Hannah. Did I do something during my pregnancy? Did we unknowingly expose her to a harmful substance when she was a baby?

Only now, in retrospect, do I see that my struggle with questions about how and why this happened was the most right and natural response I could have had to Hannah's diagnosis. It's pretty much the first and only response, I've since learned, that parents of children with regressive-nature disorders have after witnessing such abrupt changes in their child. It's literally like going from day to night. Hannah was there, and then she wasn't. So I looked long and hard for a culprit.

Then, too, I doubted my own ability to care for Hannah. Could I handle what was ahead for us? We, the doctors included, weren't even positive that Hannah *had* PDD. I remember thinking that I could spend the rest of my life raising a child who does nothing but bang her head against a wall. And what if she were to hurt me or herself? Would she ever really know I was her mom? I wasn't at all sure I was capable of this degree of sacrifice. And truthfully, I didn't want to find out.

Yes, I resented our situation. Han and I had been cheated out of our time alone with each other. We were supposed to be going to the zoo and having breakfast together. Instead, she was in school all day. I wanted things back the way they were. Poor Hannah had been through her rough times—her birth complications, her surgery—and had survived them. We didn't need this mess, this hurt.

And that's where my streaming thoughts always carried me: to the lowest point, to the core, to the hurt.

During the day, I could fill up my mind and my time with business and activity. But at night, with my body at rest, and weary from the day, the feelings flooded in. How I missed my sweet girl, her tranquil nature, her laugh, her little hands holding on to my legs while I cooked dinner. We had reached the point where she hardly paid any attention to me.

I experienced such anguish that sometimes I found myself wondering if it would have been better had Hannah's disability been evident at birth. At least we wouldn't be tortured by the memory of what used to be. And what about Hannah? Did she know what was happening to her? Did she long for her old self the way we did? My thoughts nearly drove me crazy.

But there were other factors stacked against me, too.

Charlie had always been my rock, and still was. But in his new position as offensive coordinator for the Jets, he worked around the clock. Plus he spent hours commuting between work on Long Island and our home in New Jersey. When he couldn't make it home, he slept on a portable bed in his office. Handling Hannah's situation was hard enough on him. On top of that, every night I wore him out with more worry and talk of Hannah. And, as happens in many families in our situation, things got bumpy.

I finally realized I was only adding to the weight of Charlie's load. He was in mourning, too. He had "lost" his daughter, just as I had. But he also faced the threat of losing his wife.

I backed off. The last thing Charlie needed was worry that his wife was going over the edge. So I just kept inflicting my thoughts and fears silently on myself.

I did have friends around, but no one really understood what I was going through. And out of both of our families, the only people who ever reached out or stepped up to help us were one of my nephews and my mother. Thank God my mom was with us. She'd give me a break sometimes, letting me go ride my horse, even though her radiation treatments wore her out. But I spared her from seeing my worst self. Of course, I didn't want to put any more mental strain on her; she was already burdened enough by her own poor health.

When we had lived on Long Island, I had attended a support group for parents of children with autism and PDD, but only once. Most of the parents there had older children, and they told stories without happy endings. One mother described her teenage son just staring at his upheld hand for hours and then screaming. I couldn't handle stories like that. I never went back.

When we moved to New Jersey, I assumed I'd find more of the same, so I shut the door on the idea of ever finding help in the community. I had left that first meeting so dejected and scared; I wouldn't make that mistake again.

I tried reading about various disorders and syndromes, but my mind always shifted away from the text. Next I searched the Internet but still struggled with my concentration. I didn't find the help I needed there either.

I did have little Charlie. And it was because of him that I kept it together at all. He still needed his mother. And I so needed him. Without meaning to, I hung all my hopes on him. For him, I dreamed big things. Those dreams kept me going, like the warmth from a small flame. He brought me such joy, a precious speck of stardust among the ashes. We needed each other. And so we kept each other's fires glowing, fanning and fanning when the embers got low.

It wouldn't be enough.

Months went by, and the daily discouragement I felt over Hannah's situation never subsided. It was always the same, just as she was always the same. At her new school, some children with severe PDD and autism had made great strides with their therapies. Amazingly, they seemed nearly "normal" as they moved into kindergarten. And so I had held on to the slim hope that Hannah would be there someday. But she wasn't anywhere near that point yet, at least not then. Every day she was the same when she got up in the morning. And in the middle of the night. And when she got off the school bus in the afternoon.

In fact, Hannah slipped further and further away from me, it seemed, as the weeks and the months dragged on. Once, when I was visiting Hannah's school, I just happened to cross my daughter's class in the hallway. "Hi, Hannah," I said. But she kept on walking. I waved. I smiled. The other children waved and smiled back at me. But my Hannah, she just kept walking. She didn't know who I was. She did not know her own mother.

My heart broke that day. That's when I realized that my daughter, the Hannah I once had, wasn't going to survive.

I settled into a deep and profound sadness. I told no one.

Blindly push ahead long enough, I discovered, and you'll soon find yourself alone on the path—all others swallowed up in the distance you've put between them and you. The particulars of my life had driven me into a remote outreach, and I couldn't find my way back.

In time, my isolation was complete. I became my own prisoner, immobilized and hopeless.

Driving around town with Hannah one day, I barely avoided what could have been a serious collision. I was so distracted, my mind so consumed with thoughts of Hannah, that I could hardly focus on anything else, not even driving.

In those first moments after our near miss, I realized the hold my thoughts had on me. They were relentless. And I wished I could just wipe everything out, just for a little while, just long enough to feel the briefest relief from the fear of our situation and the constant barrage of my own thoughts.

My isolation was deceptive, I later learned. Certainly I didn't get there on my own, but I made the mistake of staying. I crawled in, looking for a place to hide where my grief and longing and torment and fury and confusion wouldn't have room to find me. Someplace away from the world and all its reminders of what we had lost, away from those daily barbs and the pain. But, really, I retreated into something far worse. To refuse my suffering, I had refused life.

CHAPTER 2

TUNNELING

DOWN

I'M GRATEFUL FOR THAT CLOSE CALL IN THE CAR. It enabled me to see the utter futility of going it alone. Somehow, I knew better.

As a person of faith, I had believed in the real presence and action of the divine. God with us. The spirit immersed and suspended in all of life and everything we experience—guiding, pointing, enabling, loving. In the case of my own life, I had endured other hardships, other heartbreaks. And not on my own, I believed; God had endured them with me.

I discovered I hadn't stopped believing. So it was time I stopped running.

And once I put on the brakes, once I really looked at my situation and the impossibility of it, I knew. I needed help: help adjusting to the limitations of my marital situation, help managing my daily stresses and duties, help coping with the "restricted" life of raising a child with special needs. But before I could do any of those things, I needed to help myself. Specifically, it was time I dealt with the grieving mother in me, the person who obsessed over what "was" and agonized over what "might have been," who wrestled me out of sleep night after night yet kept me stuck in the same place, replaying the pain over and over again.

I needed to talk. "If I have to pay someone to listen, I'm going to," I told Charlie. A therapist who'd authored a couple of books I'd read years before had opened a practice nearby, so I went to him.

One hour a day, once a week, for nine months, I went. And I talked. It was the best thing I ever could have done for myself.

Something about saying the words out loud, about putting them out there in front of me—without interruption, without distraction, without judgment—gave them some form and gave me some ballast. Finally, I had something I could hold onto, unlike my cyclone thoughts that spun wildly and left me with nothing but rubble.

And as I laid out the words and the sentences and the thoughts—as I gave them some order, some sequence—I steadily worked my way through the passage, through the tunnel of my grief. Inch by inch. Word by word.

At times, the trek was hard. But I kept on, groping my way.

Dealing with my guilt was a particularly difficult part of the journey. It, I discovered, was primarily what kept me circling. With no exact cause for Hannah's condition—not even a definitive name for what it was—with no one and nothing specific to point to, I had turned my incriminations on myself. What had I done wrong during my pregnancy with Hannah? I remembered that I had contracted a virus when I was pregnant. Was that the source of Hannah's problem? And, why hadn't I gotten her ears checked sooner? Could I have stopped this from happening?

During those months of therapy, I repeatedly rehashed the lists of pregnancy "dos" and "don'ts"—didn't color my hair, didn't take medications, did gain plenty of weight—and scoured my memory for the moment when I might have slipped. I eventually concluded I hadn't done anything during my pregnancy to cause my daughter's condition. I finally gave myself a pass and quit fretting over it.

Excusing myself for not preventing Hannah's situation, though, proved much harder. As irrational and presumptuous as it may sound, I truly believed there was something I should have done to minimize Hannah's trouble. We had been so close, why hadn't I seen it coming, I repeatedly asked myself. Maybe if I had witnessed its approach, then I could have diverted the storm, kept it from reaching shore.

Because Hannah's true diagnosis eluded us, those thoughts stayed with me for years. They wouldn't remain in the therapist's office, where I tried to leave them. Much later, Charlie and I discovered that, unknown to us, Hannah had been experiencing seizures for years. There we were again, gripped by a guilt that still hasn't entirely let go.

Through the years, I have heard from so many other tormented parents struggling to work out that same thorn. Maybe tussling with guilt is just part of the progression, part of coming to terms with having a child with special needs. Somewhere down the line, though, I realized that struggling with my guilt only reminded me it was there. Better to put it away, leave it in the past. Even now, I could still beat myself up over "what I might have done." But I don't do that now, because nothing good can come of it.

As I continued to talk my way through my treatment, I eventually reached the most treacherous stretch of my journey. Getting back to some normalcy meant grappling with my hurt for Hannah. I couldn't stand thinking that our girl might never know love or happiness again. The world held abundant offerings, and I wanted Hannah to experience all of them. I longed for her to find herself breathless with laughter, silent at the sight of the ocean at dawn, awed by the towering infinity of the heavens. I wanted every good thing for her, for her life. My soul withered when I imagined that she might miss them all.

Hannah and I were both missing out. The toddler years should have been our time together. I was supposed to be her favorite playmate. We were supposed to be singing and dancing and acting silly together. And what of all those wonderful milestones in the future? Would I never see my girl scrawl out her name in red crayon, never race along beside her as she learned to ride a bike? Certainly she wasn't likely to graduate from high school. She wouldn't hold a job. I would never see her marry.

I was ashamed to admit it, but to some degree, I also felt sorry for myself. When children enter our lives, they usher in with them promise, possibility, and the chance to see the world anew. Hannah was no different. To the contrary, the little girl who had entered this world against the odds seemed to hold the universe out before us. She had made it. And so had we. It had seemed as if life's benevolences and beauty were limitless and ours for the discovering. Then came the reality of Hannah's condition, and it all seemed lost. I saw her future greatly diminished, and mine with it.

Therapy didn't extract the pain from my life. I didn't wake up one morning suddenly unaffected by my daughter's loss. But by talking things out, I learned I could manage the pain by keeping my focus on my family. It was my responsibility to give Hannah as good and as comfortable a life as I could. I had to get better—for myself, for my kids, and for Charlie. I knew that my children had noticed my withdrawal, my sadness. Charlie Jr., especially, had always been attuned to my emotional shifts and had shown a real sensitivity toward my feelings. The day I had learned of my mother's ovarian cancer, I hung up the phone crying. Charlie Jr., nearly four, ran to me shouting, "Mommy, don't cry. Mommy, don't cry. It's okay." My being upset on that occasion so disturbed him that he went into hysterics. I never cried in front of him again. While he had found two great buddies to hang out with, and he kept himself very busy for a six-year-old, I still worried about what my condition was doing to him and to our relationship. I was the parent, the post. I wanted my children to know security and stability. And I wanted to be the one to give it to them. I had no choice but to toughen up.

A part of me would always hurt for Hannah, I discovered. There would forever be that corner where the pain collected and I couldn't quite reach to sweep it away. And that was okay, I realized, as long as it stayed there. Allowing it any more space in my world would only diminish Hannah's life and the life of our family.

I concluded my therapy with one simple but brilliant insight. However bad the hurt, it could never blot out my love for my daughter. Nothing could touch that. That light was simply too strong.

With that one thought, I felt unleashed, set loose in my life again. Grief did not own me. It never had, never would. I rejoiced! And I marveled at love's amazing power.

"Hannah will be okay," that voice had told me years before when I was pregnant with my daughter. And once again, I knew it to be true. Our life together would be fabulous, whatever it entailed. However, no power of my own positive thinking could have convinced me of that. God, the source of love, had brought Hannah and me together and sealed our bond forever. And I had had to step back and allow myself to receive from God and others. With help came revelation.

As parents, I believe, we're given a wonderful charge: to raise our children up in love. It's a tremendous gift and a daunting challenge. But once we're given the responsibility, it's ours. If God had entrusted Charlie and me with a special needs child, I reasoned, then maybe it was because we, specifically, could provide for all her special needs. Yes, she would have more challenges, but maybe we also came ready-made to help her with everything she would face. God knew what we were made of and were capable of, I decided. We would not be set up to fail. Through the years, as I came to know parents of children with Asperger's syndrome, autism, Down syndrome, cerebral palsy, and a host of other challenges, I found this inkling to be accurate. Parents who raise children with special needs possess a little something special in them, too.

What I learned from my bout with depression was that I had to prepare for the long race ahead. In my case, the therapy pulled me out and enabled me to set a course for my family and me. I can't suggest therapy for everyone just because of what I went through. But typically, parents experiencing a similar loss do need to find help somewhere. For some, local support groups help them through. Others seek out meditation, yoga, individual and family counseling, a priest or rabbi, exercise, Internet chat rooms, even medication. I don't think the means matters.

When the walls close in, when life seems squeezed and minimal, find help. Grab hold of the walls and climb your way up. Find the crawlspaces and the cracks in the floor. Dig in your nails and pry open the seams at the corners.

Wherever there is help, get to it. Whatever it takes, do it.

For me, just getting to the therapist was like winning the prizefight. Once I allowed myself to accept help—from a therapist, as well as from God—I recognized the bounty of resources available to me. Some were physical, some spiritual. But because I knew they were there, I never approached a challenge the same way again. And there were many more challenges. There still are.

With newfound resolve, my family and I developed a team mentality and approach to our situation. (Yes, we describe it in terms of a "team"!) In a family, working together seems as though it ought to be a given. But often it's not, so it takes effort, just as a marriage takes effort.

Luckily, we already had a lot of good things going for us. Most importantly, there were two parents. As hard as things had been for me, I couldn't imagine raising two children, one with special needs, on my own. Some single parents can do it—and do it well—while still keeping it together themselves. I take my hat off to them;

they really have to do double the work. But, on the whole, I'd venture to guess, it's a less-than-ideal situation. Speaking from my own experience, having that second person around, that partner to pull you out of the tight spots, proves essential.

But Charlie and I were realists: we knew that our marriage's odds for survival weren't good. We'd heard a statistic that in families with special needs children, up to 80 percent of marriages split up. With those odds, couples need to do all they can to tip the scales in their favor. We were no exception.

For instance, under any other circumstances, Charlie never would have recommended that I go to therapy. But because he loved me and wanted the best for me, it was important to him that I found the help I needed. I've always been grateful for that.

With work, we steered away from the blame game and avoided keeping score. And that's tough in any marriage. When we moved back to New Jersey, Charlie came home only twice a week during the season. The good coaches often put in more than a hundred hours a week in pro football jobs, and Charlie had the added commute. Charlie's absences got me down at times, for sure. He's a fantastic husband and father, and I would always prefer that he be with us. But I understood the demands of his job; I couldn't hold them against him.

For our situation to work, we had to trust each other's choices and judgments and learn from the results. Of course, Charlie and I both had our "that's-not-how-I-would-have-called-it" moments. But because we were wholly committed to making Hannah's life, as well as our family's life, as good as possible, we refused to stay hung up on petty irritations or hold on to our grievances. We spoke our minds, we listened, we learned, and we moved on.

It's a mantra I'd recommend for any relationship. It makes giving easier. Rarely did I ever hear Charlie complain about being tired, not even in the middle of the season, when he was working so many hours. The nights he came home, he'd pull up at some ridiculous hour, after reviewing videotape all night, and then stay up for hours with our little night owl. The next morning, he'd haul himself out the door again and head into another sixteen-hour day. There was little to no grumbling about it, at least not that I heard. Charlie just did things like that. We both did.

But part of "doing what needed to be done" included preserving our time together as a couple. Throughout Charlie Jr.'s infancy and toddler years, Charlie and I had kept a date night once a week. We had tried to continue that practice when Hannah came into our lives, although any consistency went by the boards. Still, the occasional times when we did go to dinner together were always worth the effort. Those times away from the children gave us a glimpse of the life we had previously shared, and we really enjoyed them. They reminded us that we weren't cut off from the rest of the world, not completely. We'd return home with our spirits lifted.

It was also good for our kids to see us together. I'm sure that with all the upheaval Charlie Jr. had experienced—the frequent moves, a changed sister, a distracted mother, and a father who was home rather infrequently because of his job—our presence together, and the time we spent alone with him, provided him some much-needed reassurance. Over the years, I've seen so many children displaced by their parents' all-consuming concern over a child with special needs. It's as if the parents have forgotten that their other children have needs, too. And though parents may not realize it, such an approach also discourages the child with special needs from finding his or her own independence. In the realm of disabilities, the "goal" should always be to help this child or adult become as independent as possible. While an obsession with the child with special needs is an obvious yet common pitfall, we're thankful that we learned to avoid it. If anything, I'd say we sharpened our awareness of Charlie Jr.'s feelings, taking extra precautions to make sure he never felt brushed aside or left behind. In the middle of our discovery of Hannah's condition, I had deliberately kept him out of preschool. I hadn't wanted him feeling we had shipped him out. But then our son was never the sort to let us forget he was still around. It wasn't in his personality or his makeup. When he wanted attention, he made sure he got it. If he thought I had been with Hannah too long, he'd say, "Mommy, Hannah had enough time now. She's sleepy. It's time for my time."

But just as much as I needed individual time with my husband and my son, I also needed time for myself. I learned to work it in, making time for coffee with a friend or getting myself out to the barn. It was crucial that I put myself somewhere different than the house. For me, the barn was that place where I could temporarily break out of my routines and my role. The barn and my horses were and remain my great escape. The earthy scent, the sight of the horses in their paddocks or grazing was enough to help me slow down and reengage those aspects of my being that had been neglected or pushed aside. At the barn, people didn't talk kids or football. There, I got in touch with the rest of me again.

One of my favorite horses, a gray Arabian named Mystic, was a spooky, nervous sort. Riding her required every ounce of my concentration. I couldn't let my mind slip off into the latest Hannah issue, or Charlie's press coverage, or even what we were eating for dinner that night. When I rode, it was just the horse and me.

And really, riding was prayer. I can think of no other way to describe those moments when I'm fully absorbed by an activity. The spirit resonates within me, the horse, the air. Bent knees guide the horse's middle, hands fold firmly around the reins.

I have always been fond of horses, their nobility and mystery. The ancient Greeks claimed that God thought long and hard before giving horses to humans, and I know why. Horses speak an unspoken language that I feel I can understand because I make a point of listening. To me, all creatures hold a place of significance in the world, because I regard them all as visible inclinations of the divine. Riding my horse puts me in touch with God, nourishing and sustaining me.

Despite some of the positive changes we were making, I still didn't sleep much, what with Hannah's nightly escapades. But I did alter one habit that, in the early days after Hannah's initial diagnosis, had consumed a lot of my downtime: surfing the Internet. Every night, like clockwork, Hannah would go to bed, and I'd go online. Besides depriving myself of much-needed rest, I found information that terrified me. And what I was reading online kept my mind racing on and on through the night. It's an easy trap to fall into. I wanted to help my child, so I had to get to the bottom of our mystery and solve it by discovering an answer.

In my new plan, I still diligently pursued answers and advice. But I limited my time on the computer and became more discriminating about the sites I chose and the times of day I did my digging. Eventually, I sought out people a little more and the Internet a little less.

With the help of others, I moved beyond the fear and the debilitating sorrow that had limited me and threatened my family. And over some time, much beyond my months of therapy, I learned to accept my feelings of disappointment. What loving parent wouldn't feel let down, I conceded. I got better at dealing with the disappointments themselves.

Raising a child with special needs *is* tough. Brace for it. There will be moments—months—when the horizon dulls, as hopes and prospects seem to fade away. Sometimes, it appears, the road goes nowhere. But if we, as parents, stop looking ahead, stop expecting, stop exploring, what *will* we see? And to what will we lead our children?

We all deserve to hope, to anticipate, to experience life's happiness. Maybe Hannah never would in the same way, but what chance did she stand for any kind of future if *I* didn't feel hopeful? We invite our children, and everything they bring with them, into our lives. So we embark on the road together, hand in hand, to see what we will see. When we raise a child with special needs, the expanses and vistas are different, true enough. But, as I discovered, the views are no less grand.

I had drifted far from myself to the point where I had forgotten who I was, who I was called to be. But the God I once believed to reside and work and move in all things, I found, still resided, still worked, and still moved in all things. That included me. And I realized for the first time since we became aware of Hannah's challenges that God worked in her too, for she had brought me here, into this new realm of faith, this new room of love.

Hannah had changed in many ways from the way I remembered her. But in one way, she hadn't changed. She was still a reflection of the divine, one glimmer in the jewel of creation. Like everyone, like every thing, she was a part of it all—that would never change. Not even in death. In all the magnificence of the cosmos, her light shone too, a pinpoint of white at the end of a tunnel.

CHAPTER 3

TRUSTING

MY

INSTINCTS

I ANSWERED THE PHONE. IT WAS AN OLD FRIEND of mine whom I had spent a lot of time with when I was in my twenties. We had stayed in touch, and I had kept her updated on Hannah's situation. And once or twice a week, we'd connect by phone. But on this particular day Hannah had bolted when the phone rang. At first I thought nothing of it, but after a few moments she hadn't come back. It suddenly occurred to me that the escape was deliberate. She knew: Mom was tied up.

"I've gotta get off the phone," I told my friend. "I don't know where Hannah is; she's not around me."

I hung up and headed for the living room. No Hannah. The foyer. Not there either. I eyed the staircase. I ran for it and dashed my way up, two steps at a time.

At the top, I could not believe my eyes. Our ivory-carpeted hallway was a mess. And the damage didn't stop there. The floor in Hannah's bedroom, the walls, her wicker furniture, her toys, all were splattered and smeared with diarrhea. Filth and smell covered Hannah too. Her diaper lay in a wretched, stinky wad on the floor. And there sat Hannah, looking at me as if nothing had happened.

I was enraged. Hannah was three and a half. How could this have happened? How could she do this? I had never been so angry; I wanted to spank her. A bloodcurdling scream was poised to erupt from my throat.

I choked it back and dived into the bathroom. I set Hannah in the empty tub and proceeded to clean up the mess.

To call this my meltdown moment would be an absurd understatement. More accurately, this was my moment of implosion, when every cell in my body ignited with rage and frustration, short-circuiting the breaker and sending me crashing in on myself. "What am I supposed to do?" I said out loud. "I don't know what I'm going to do!"

And because I didn't know, I just kept cleaning doo-doo off the doorjamb, the baseboard, the door-knob. And I just kept talking. "If this is a test," I angrily announced to God, "I'm passing this one too!"

I checked on Hannah, then went back to cleaning some more. I wiped crap off doll faces, the laundry hamper, the rug.

Back to Hannah, sitting blissfully unaware. Back to the mess. To Hannah again. Then the mess.

It took me a good hour to clean up Hannah and the house. The ivory carpet was stained. But other than that, no real damage.

I took some deep breaths and realized that, in the midst of my crisis, I *had* known what to do. Or maybe, to be more accurate, my body knew what to do. It had already been a rough week for me, and I had had it. My frustration level had topped out, and this incident had pushed me past my limit. I had had nowhere to go, so I had folded.

But surprisingly, my world did not come flying apart. Instead, I simply found myself at the bottom, the beginning. Base camp. There, it's only about dealing with the crisis of the moment. That's all there is, nothing else. At this station, there is only the moment; the intimidating view of the mountain face is obscured. It has to be, or we'd never deal with the crisis, let alone take the first step toward climbing back up.

I tangibly felt an internal repositioning. Faced with a daughter and a house covered in filth, I forced all other concerns aside. If the phone rang, I didn't hear it. Fundraiser for Hannah's school? Hadn't thought about it. Single-mindedly, I rolled up my sleeves and set about furiously soaping, scrubbing, and sanitizing the problem in front of me. Mental breakdown averted by the brain's quick switch of the tracks.

When the cleanup was all finished, I looked at Hannah and realized she had no idea what she had done. One of the medical reports we received had said this might happen, that children with conditions similar to Hannah's often smeared excrement. I felt bad for my girl. She spent every day of her life in pain. If it wasn't stomach cramps, it was the diarrhea, which burned and irritated her skin. Of course she had pitched her diaper, I thought, she's sick and tired of this too. We were on common ground.

That day something turned over in me. With no solution in sight at the time, I realized that Hannah might have diarrhea for the rest of her life. And for the rest of my life, I might be cleaning it up. On that day, I knew for sure that my life would be different forever. And that this might be what it was all about.

I had been through therapy, had worked my way through my grief, had devised a plan of action and care for my family. But not until that day, that incident, did I acknowledge my "lot" with such clarity. There was still the possibility that Hannah would improve; I didn't let go of that dream. But something inside me told me I was in it for the long haul.

I wasn't the same after that day. I was better. With no end to our difficult situation in sight, I discovered the ability to approach my life day by day, moment by moment. And with that realigned perspective, any incident like this with Hannah was just that: one incident, nothing more. The spilled soda, just a spilled soda. A nosebleed, just one nosebleed. A fit in a public place, one fit, one place. Graciously, God had taught me the art of reduction. Simplification by taking life one moment at a time.

Raising Hannah has taught me to deal with things as they arise. There is no point in dreading what else is headed our way during the course of a day; we have no idea. And there is no sense whining about the way things are; that just makes things worse. There will be challenges, problems—lots of them—but they will emerge naturally over the course of time. And as a human being, I am obliged to follow the course. Running the long race means reserving my energy. Doling it out piecemeal helps preserve my attitude and my sanity.

Parenthood is hard: the change in lifestyle, the shift in expectations, the new demands on time, the separation from the previous self. It's as if you are plucked right up out of your old life and set down in a new one—where friends without kids drop by less often, where the mail carrier delivers baby formula coupons instead of *Cosmo*, where sleep and showers come at a premium. And let's not forget the overarching fear: Am I doing this right?

Consider, then, the concerns facing those of us who are parents of a child with a disability or a threatening illness. In our case, since we really didn't know definitely what was "wrong" with Hannah and since she didn't fit neatly into any disability category (meaning it could have been anything), we could have easily worried about everything. At times, I did.

It started soon after we were first aware of Hannah's challenges and condition. I couldn't contain my nervousness. I exercised to work off stress. I sought the solace and comfort of nature. But still, I was jumpy. I had already given birth to and was raising another child, but Charlie Jr. did not have special needs. I felt dangerously unprepared for raising Hannah because we didn't know what we were dealing with. A friend of mine used to tell me I looked like a deer caught in headlights. And that's exactly how I felt.

Even now, the nervousness about parenting Hannah still lives with me. And to a degree, I think, that's okay. It doesn't rule my life anymore. But I would question my worth as a parent if I did not feel some prick of cautionary concern for my children. And though there have been moments through the years when my anxiety erupts and takes over again, it doesn't stick around for long. I know how much better my life is without being anxious.

That's why finding "me time" is so imperative for any parent of a child with special needs. If you're uncomfortable leaving a child with someone, don't leave the house. Go out in the yard, plant yourself in a quiet room and read a book, grab an hour for a nap. Finding the calm benefits both parents and kids.

I diffused myself by caring for and riding my horse and by talking. I didn't join a support group or meet with the moms from Hannah's school. I talked to God. I talked to my ancestors. I even talked to a little bird named Pidgey. When Charlie Jr. was about six, I bought him a pet cockatiel. The relationship was short-lived. Pidgey pooped on my son, and that was that. So Pidgey hung out with me. At night, when Charlie was away, I'd spill everything to that little bird. As much as any trained practitioner, Pidgey provided good therapy. He never judged me. And for seven years, he was a faithful listener. Though he passed on, he visits me in my dreams. There are days when I still feel his quieting presence on my shoulder.

Prayer also grounds me. To me, prayer is a conversation. Sometimes I initiate dialogue, sometimes God does, sometimes it's the people whose existence also allowed me a place on this planet. There's a channel, a cord that connects us all, that binds together all of creation, really. So, I believe, that when I call out, when I seek help, when I am overcome with praising, my utterances aren't swallowed up into nothing. They are received. And when I am struck by a vision, a song, a memory, a thought, it is God and the spirit of my ancestors who reach out to me. I have learned to receive. I look and listen for guides.

During the toughest years, and even beyond them, I could rely on an old friend of mine to give

me a boost when I needed it. Brenda, a dear friend
who had worked with me in Manhattan, called or
stopped over nearly every day. She always offered
words that encouraged me and lifted me up. She
was my cheerleader. So many times I've wondered
what would have happened if Brenda hadn't
reached out to me so often.

Brenda would hear me out as I caught her up
on our family's story. Then she'd tell me how
great I was doing and pour on the compliments.
"What mom would do that for her child?" she'd
say. "Hannah is so lucky to have you." It worked.
Every mom, with a special needs child or not, can
use a cheerleader like Brenda.

Don't be surprised if the cheerleader or the listener isn't someone or something you'd expect.
Pidgey, for instance. On the other hand, don't be
too disappointed if people you thought would
always be around gradually slip out of your life. I
never would have imagined that some family
members would grow so distant. Nor could I
believe the words that fell out of a dear friend's
mouth while she was visiting Hannah and me one

day. The occasion was a day like any other, with good moments and bad. Hannah had gotten upset about something and had started screaming and crying loudly. When peace resumed, my friend looked at me and asked, "How do you love that?" I haven't spoken to her since.

Yes, the diarrhea incident prepared me for many things. People, I learned, came and went. And tough times too. I haven't tossed in the towel or traded in my hopes for Hannah. But there's something to be said for yielding to the reality of life.

Of course, it all got easier with time. The more you do something, the more customary and routine it becomes. I learned that poop cleans up just as easy with soap and water as with any special stain remover. And when the phone rang, I made sure I grabbed the cordless. With one messy incident, Hannah had pushed me way past my limits, so I was forced to extend my boundaries. And from that, we all benefited.

I had found a new level of comfort with our situation, and in doing so, I also unearthed a strength, a boldness, for dealing with Hannah's physical and emotional concerns. And I realized more clearly than ever before that no one else could care for Hannah as well as I could.

The day of Hannah's "accident," I was still angry after I had finished cleaning up the mess. I wasn't angry at Hannah, but at my friend. She hadn't forcibly fixed the phone to my ear, but when I had tried to get off the line, she had kept talking. I had hung up anyway. But the fact that she had kept right on talking really bothered me. Maybe she hadn't heard me or picked up on the concern in my voice. Maybe she had thought I was overreacting. Or maybe she just hadn't cared where Hannah was. How odd, I had thought. She was a mom. She should have known that her attempt at delaying me wasn't merely discourteous but showed a real disregard for me and the safety of my child.

Later I realized she really didn't know. She didn't "get it" at all. None of my closest friends at that time had children with disabilities. We lived in completely different worlds. They didn't have to lock up the cupboards or tie off the fridge with a rope to keep their child from overeating. And for them, a trip to the grocery store with their kids was nothing. For us, it was a major production. We never knew how Hannah would react. If she had a meltdown in the store, then I spent all my time calming her and trying to ignore looks from other shoppers. I had already lost count of the times we had returned home empty-handed.

And friends with and without kids would call to ask if Hannah and I wanted to go to the mall or catch a movie. I knew, in some cases, that people's hearts were in the right place. Some wanted Hannah to feel included. But others were just clueless. They seemed to forget what I had told them about Hannah's discomfort in crowds. Sometimes that obliviousness irritated me.

Certainly other mothers of children with special needs, like the parents at Hannah's school, could empathize with our situation; they had some idea of what we were experiencing. And this did help. But really, our situation was uniquely our own because Hannah was uniquely Hannah.

And since I knew her best, no one would or ever could do better by her than I could.

That confidence equipped me for some tough battles. But it also revived a reluctance to count on others for help. Leaving Hannah with a sitter, even though I had two exceptional ones, still made me uneasy. I knew my limitations. I did not know anyone else's. I could handle the Hannah crises and tolerate her challenging behaviors because I had learned how and because I loved her. What did strangers possess to allow them to do the same? And how would they know her needs? Eventually I found a balance: caution tempered with faith in the good people who made their way into our lives.

My confidence in trusting my own instincts grew, and I knew I wouldn't allow Hannah to suffer on with her diarrhea. But I also knew I would have to be the one to find the cure. I resumed my hunt with new resolve.

First, I took Hannah to her pediatrician, who suggested that Hannah take Imodium on a daily basis. His suggestion made no sense to me.

Shouldn't we be tackling the source of the problem, I thought, not just the messy side effect? I felt as if I had gotten the brushoff, as if Hannah were considered a "lost cause." Unfortunately, this wouldn't be the only time I felt this way.

I would be negligent not to warn other parents and caregivers of children with special needs about this. While there are many fine doctors in the world, I have gotten the clear impression that some of Hannah's doctors gave her less than their all. To me, they presented an attitude of "Your daughter is not right. She never will be right, so what's the point?" The fact that Hannah could not verbalize her symptoms didn't help matters. Many doctors seemed to lack the patience for pursuing the cause of Hannah's problems, as if they just weren't up for the challenge. Certainly, it's crossed my mind that doctors would not have shown the same reservation or conservatism in treating my son or their own children. While I've been discouraged by that thought at times, I've always fallen back on the obvious. I am *the* one. It will always be me, until I die. Hannah's well-being, at least regarding decisions for her health, is in my hands. Ultimately, I make the choices.

I hit the Internet again and this time found information on celiac disease—an allergy to wheat and gluten that affects the digestive system. That, I thought, could be Hannah's problem. I took her in to have her intestines 'scoped. At first, the doctor told me Hannah did have celiac disease. But a biopsy showed otherwise. I was back at square one.

Several months later, the mom of one of Hannah's classmates put me on to her son's wheat-free, gluten-free, organic diet. It had worked like a miracle for him. By eating different foods, Hannah's classmate went from being basically incommunicative to attending a mainstream kindergarten. It was nothing short of incredible.

I checked with Hannah's pediatrician, who assured me that the dietary change wouldn't harm her. So we gave it a try. It wasn't easy switching Hannah to her new diet at first. She loved her chicken nuggets and chocolate shakes, and she let us know she wasn't at all happy that she was no longer getting them, but she eventually adjusted. And while I was told it might take a year to see any significant health changes in Hannah, in only three days her diarrhea was significantly less. I was sold.

The payoff was more than we had expected. Though it didn't go away completely, Hannah's diarrhea improved, which meant decreased stomach pain and skin irritation. And with less pain, Hannah started sleeping through the night more often. And because she slept more, Hannah was less tired, less agitated, less grumpy during the day. And that made the days easier for both of us. Who would have guessed that one crappy incident on an ivory carpet could spur such good? It was my cue to keep looking.

As parents, we are the best (and sometimes the only) advocates for our children. Yes, we do need to rely on others for their experience, wisdom, and training. And their support. Where would we be if I hadn't talked to the mother who had put her son on the organic diet? But by the same token, where would we be if I had followed a doctor's orders and put Hannah on anti-diarrhea medicine for life? Doctors, therapists, nutritionists, and other medical experts all know a great deal and have a lot to show us. But, still, their views are limited.

The day-to-day management of a child's life and well-being belongs to the parents and other primary caregivers. They are the ones passing hour after hour with their children. They are the ones sitting at the bedside. They are the ones who know exactly what their children think, or feel, or want, sometimes without the prompt of one spoken word.

I had to learn how to get a child with hypersensitive gums to brush her teeth every day. I had to learn to bring notes and a list of questions to every one of Hannah's medical appointments. I had to learn how to settle down a hysterical child with a whopper of a nosebleed.

In the same way, I learned to differentiate between what might be good for Hannah and what was best for her. I had always been the kind to heed my inner voice. And as I raised Hannah, I found the frequency of that voice, and my tendency to follow it, intensified. My instincts—guided by those whom I sought in prayer, I believe—proved a reliable compass.

A few years down the road, as Hannah approached adolescence and her hormones kicked in, she had trouble sleeping again. Still, I would send her off to school in the morning despite the fact that she seemed tired and reluctant to go. It seemed like the thing to do at the time. She needed her therapy and loved seeing her friends and teachers. But then I realized I was not improving the quality of her life, or her school day, by sending her to school without the rest she needed. I knew Hannah preferred being on a schedule, but my instincts told me that she didn't have to adhere to one strictly. She was okay with some change; there was some room for flux. I decided to let her sleep in when she needed to. If it meant that Hannah would be happier and enjoy herself more, then it was okay with me if she went to school late. Hannah's happiness was, after all, my primary concern.

To some, this event and others like it may sound like typical, everyday parental shot calling, and that's because they are. But to me, they are also small victories, proof I have grown and am growing into my role as parent of a child who has special needs. They show I am not becoming rigid, even though hard-and-fast schedules offer their own kind of comfort in the face of so much that is unknown. I am not running in every direction. I am finding my own compass. They are notches in my belt, hash marks denoting Hannah's and my progress. They encourage me. Therefore I feel they must be benevolently directed.

At one point, I felt a strong urge to have Hannah examined by a geneticist. The PDD diagnosis had never set well with me, and after more than a year of research, I was even less sold on it. Things were going well with Hannah, but they could be better, I thought. I wanted to nail down Hannah's real diagnosis. Maybe there was something we could be doing for her that we weren't doing already. Maybe there was a therapy or a treatment that could ease things up for her a bit.

The geneticist confirmed my doubts: Hannah did not fall into the category of PDD, but instead presented global developmental delays. Pervasive developmental disorders are characterized, in part, by impaired reciprocal social interaction and communication skills. Global delays, however, imply a lag in all developmental criteria, including speech and language, social skills, and gross and fine motor skills.

Years later, after noticing changes in Hannah's physical appearance, I took her to another geneticist. We were informed Hannah had developed slight mental retardation brought on by seizures. Not what we wanted to hear, no doubt, but something we had to know. We got her on anti-seizure medication, which also curbed her appetite and enabled her to sleep more soundly through the night.

To date, Hannah has seen three geneticists and five neurologists in our attempts at uncovering her true diagnosis. While we believe, now, that we have found an answer, research and medicine are continually advancing, so I persist in my search regardless. That's not to say I spend every waking hour seeking an answer. But where there's a stone, I eventually turn it over.

Then again, as any parent in this situation will attest, you can't always know for certain what's going on with your child's health. A parent might be able to detect the onset of depression, but something less obvious emotionally or physically may prove to be a more difficult discovery. For example, when Hannah was about nine she was diagnosed with scoliosis. But only after she'd worn the corrective back brace a while did we discover her plastic allergy, and only because we saw her scratching her arms. A blood test revealed not only Hannah's allergy to plastic, but lo and behold, also an allergy to cotton. So, we wondered, could our daughter's cute cotton jammies be partly to blame for keeping her up at night? We switched her over to silk and polyester, and sure enough, we were all sleeping easier.

Putting a finger on our daughter's health issues has been a frustrating game of hit and miss, in part because Hannah can't always alert us to the problems she's having. That's also why I watch, I hunt, I question. In recent years, I've even started taking the nutritional supplements that Hannah receives. I'm not suggesting that others take up this practice, but it's part of what I do to know my daughter and to share her experiences.

I encourage all parents to know their children first, and then to listen to and trust their gut. If a treatment or a diagnosis or a therapy seems like too much or not enough, seek an alternative. Extend the boundaries and dig. And know that sometimes, temporarily or for good, we have to put down the shovel.

Raising a child with special needs doesn't have to be a test of endurance or a trip to martyrdom. But being the parent I want to be, and helping my daughter experience the kind of life I think she'd like to have, does mean moving forward with deliberation. It's meeting up with challenges as they arise, every day. It's not bemoaning, "Why Hannah?" or "Why me?" And it's not conceding defeat. It's devising a new plan.

There still are days when I feel helplessly over-whelmed. And given the nature of our situation, it's bound to happen. I don't feel bad about that. For the most part, I do try to live one day at a time. In those moments when I crumble, I am humbled. And I soundly remind myself that it's only because God is with me that I have the ability to do this at all. I also come out of these experiences grateful they don't happen more often. And some-times, just sometimes, I rise up out of them a little stronger than I was before.

No one knows my daughter better than I do. She is with me every day. She is my daily ritual. I pass my days preparing her meals and laying out her clothes. Wiping food from her face; cleaning her hands. Running her bath water. Washing her hair. Toweling off her body. By being present to each of these daily interactions, they draw me in, bring me ever nearer to the source of strength and hope, to the soul, to Hannah. And to the common ground we all share that is beyond this world.

CHAPTER 4

FINDING

OUR

DAUGHTER

I USED TO TALK TO A PICTURE OF HANNAH YEARS ago. The photo depicts my daughter, just over a year old, wearing her favorite red and white striped dress. She's smiling, her dimpled elbow peeping out from beneath her sleeve. She has just swung open a dresser door and pulled herself up beside it. And I caught her at the moment she turned to see if I was watching. She is so pleased, with herself, with me, with life. Her eyes reveal the laughter that swells in her heart.

I kept that photo close by me so that when I missed Hannah the most, I could pull it out and talk to the girl I once knew. "I'm gonna get you back," I would tell the little girl in the photo, and then I would address Hannah herself. "You're in there, and you're going to come back to me. I'm going to do everything I can to get you back."

It was a prayer lofted into creation, words ferrying the desire of my heart out to the universe. For years I stared at that photo and uttered my promise, my plea. To stop, I thought then, would have meant I'd given up on my girl. I felt I owed it to the "old" Hannah to do all I could to retrieve her.

And so it was my earnest undertaking to find "the solution" to our problem. I worked to make Hannah's life in the present better, more comfortable, freer, happier. But at the same time, I still sought the spell that would make all things right again. I had to, I thought then, to remain true to the daughter I once knew. Though Hannah's future seemed set, I couldn't close the door completely. It was okay to hold on to my hope, I decided. Miracles happen.

When Hannah was five, a cyst developed on her remaining kidney. Again, surgery was an option, but the doctor suggested we wait to see if more cysts developed, possibly indicating polycystic kidney disease, which Hannah had been diagnosed with in the womb. Both Charlie and I were relieved to be able to defer, if temporarily, the option of another operation. Our little girl had already been through so much. Yes, waiting seemed just fine to us.

During those weeks and months that passed, I researched and explored various alternative medicine treatments for Hannah. One in particular grabbed my attention, and I pursued it. Reiki, a holistic therapy, is thought to free up the energy flow in the body, allowing it to help heal itself.

The practice's concepts resonate with me. Raised Catholic, I grew up accepting the mystery that is faith, that is life. We, too, are part of the mystery, composed of more than what can be seen or touched or measured. The spirit abides in and around us all, I believe, and we experience this most clearly through the natural world. These beliefs still permeate all the corners of my life, including my views on medicine and health care.

Charlie, to say the least, was less sold on the idea. But when I found a reiki healer in our area who was also a Catholic nun, it all seemed providential.

How could we refuse? Over the next several months, Sister Claudine performed the soothing ritual on our daughter. Once or twice a week, she entered our home, laid her spirit-guided hands on Hannah, and recited her words of healing.

At Hannah's six-year wellness appointment, no new growths had developed on her kidney. But better yet, the original cyst was gone. I felt renewed and affirmed. It was right that I had kept my mind open to new approaches. This was clearly a remarkable healing; maybe there would be more.

Hannah kept on with school and therapy, and I continued to be her caretaker. We got through our days pretty well together. Hannah loved music, so we'd watch Barney videos in the afternoon. And any time she was home, I sang to her. The Barney songs were her favorites, and despite my terrible voice, I would sing to Hannah whenever we were together. Always the same songs, over and over again. She couldn't get enough. To her, my voice was beautiful. So I kept singing.

It was a good practice to keep up. My singing calmed Hannah when she was afraid or uncertain. It helped both of us gain our composure when we felt angry or frustrated. And if things were sailing along happily, the singing just naturally reflected the mood.

Hannah's speech therapists also had always sung to Hannah often, a practice intended to encourage Hannah's speech. In every session, the therapists launched into "Twinkle, Twinkle, Little Star," their hands opening and closing in time with the music, simulating a twinkling heavenly body. Then one day, Hannah surprised everyone at the session by answering the therapist's lilting, singsong voice with her own sweet falsetto. "The stars are in the sky," she sang. I was not around to hear it, but it didn't matter. My heart sang. It was one of the few sentences that my daughter had ever spoken. After the session, the thought of Hannah's clear, melodic voice resounded in my ears for hours. It was beautiful.

Of course, there was a time or two when Hannah's words were not as nice. During one of

Hannah's first days at a new school, she got her foot stuck in the playground fence. She let loose with, "Shit!" Of course, when her teacher told me, I was embarrassed. Of all the things she could have said, it had to be that, I thought. She was with me all the time, everyone knew, so where else could she have heard it? I was busted. But her teacher and I both laughed over it. It was cool, I later thought, that Hannah had known when to drop her bomb. She had spoken a word, that was good. But using it appropriately, that was great.

While raising our daughter, Charlie and I discovered that Hannah was tuned into us in ways that others simply couldn't recognize. She watched us and read our moods. She memorized our living patterns, modeled our behaviors. And she knew how to work us.

When we managed to resist her heart-melting gaze, not giving in to another piece of chocolate cake or potato chips, she'd move on to Plan B: bugging us. When we still wouldn't budge, it was Plan C: something crafty. Sometimes Hannah would sit stealthily in the next room, patiently waiting for the moment when the kitchen was all clear. Then she'd move furniture to boost herself up to the cabinet that held the goodies. Or, better still, she'd come charging in when the phone rang, knowing that Mommy would give her a treat to keep her quiet. Though it wore us out, her persistence grew endearing. Not quitting was a family trait. Without a doubt, she was our girl.

No, Hannah was not at all absent. From the outside, it may have appeared as if she were vacant, impenetrable. Yet as we raised her, we began to learn all that was firing away in her mind. More significantly, though, we discovered the person, the soul, who resided within Hannah.

Hannah, like all human beings, was distinctly herself. Some of her traits and behaviors were learned; some, like her stubbornness, inherited. But there were also parts of Hannah that were all her and only her. And as the years passed, the gift of Hannah unfolded before us.

Until she was about seven years old, Hannah had a thing for young, good-looking guys. Anytime she'd spot the handsome new gym teacher at school, she'd make a beeline for him. Charlie and I got a kick out of it. Then came the school's Christmas pageant. Hannah didn't have a speaking or singing part, but she looked absolutely adorable wearing her red velvet dress and standing by her aide. After the show, the kids all lined up to visit Santa Claus. When it was Hannah's turn, she plopped herself down on Santa's lap, reached up, and yanked the beard right off the cute gym teacher. None of the other kids had known Santa's true identity, but Hannah could not be fooled.

It was just one of the many things that made Hannah special. And through the years, we developed a real fondness for her ways. Things that might disturb or upset parents of other children didn't faze us. To us, they were what made Hannah Hannah.

I remember that when Hannah was preschool age, she enjoyed walking around the house with a bucket on her head. For some parents, that would be tough to take. But to our family, it was humorous, in a "there she goes again" sort of way. We'd all be in the basement, playing Nintendo with Charlie Jr., and Hannah would be bumping about with her bucket. For whatever reason, she liked it, and we were fine with that.

And she loved it whenever a birthday cake showed up at the house. It didn't have to be her birthday cake, just anybody's. She'd park herself right next to it and wait for a piece. It wouldn't matter if she'd already had one. It was cake, and she was sticking close by. Once I found her asleep next to her favorite frosted food, but even that wasn't all that unusual. With her interrupted sleep patterns, Hannah crashed whenever and wherever fatigue caught up with her. We have plenty of memories of her snoozing next to her cereal bowl or catching a nap in the middle of her afternoon snack. The thought of those times still makes me smile.

Then, for a while, Hannah disliked wearing clothes. It's a common trait among kids with sensory issues. And because being dressed bothered her, we allowed Hannah to walk around in nothing but her underwear. When we were still living in New Jersey, Charlie Jr.'s friends would come over to play, and Hannah, then four, wouldn't care that she wasn't dressed. In fact, neither would Charlie and I. Charlie Jr., his friends, and his friends' parents didn't mind either. In the world we had created around her, Hannah was accepted for who she was. The experience was new to us, and it was liberating. My husband, my son, and I had all grown more comfortable with the "new" Hannah. Time saw to that. Also, we had a core group of neighbors and friends who were good to us. I wondered if they had known other special needs individuals or if they were simply imitating the way that we treated Hannah. In other words, were they okay with Hannah because *we* were okay with Hannah? Either way, the sensitivity shown to us, to our daughter, set us even more at ease. And I was reminded, once again, of the thread that ties us to one another and of the delicate exchange of invest and return. Put love out there, and it's certain to come back around.

I also think that children from birth are gifted with the ability to disregard the exterior packaging of people. They just look right through what adults would call a disability or special needs. All they see is the essence of the individual. I like to think that Charlie Jr.'s friends saw Hannah's true essence, and that is why we were all so comfortable together.

How I wish we could all hold on to that perception. It's a radical way of seeing, of living. Jesus exemplified it when he talked to the Samaritan woman at the well, when he broke bread with tax collectors and believers alike, when he healed those of great and little faith. In our lives, Hannah has helped us recognize the value in every person. And through the years, our frame of reference has gradually shifted. Our focus adjusted.

I have a list of ten personal goals I meditate on daily. Among them are "Don't judge others; you don't know their story" and "Love like there is no tomorrow." These two goals are interwoven—one follows the other. Both are especially poignant for us. Both teach us valuable lessons. But the second we've learned the hard way: life is too short.

With Hannah's diagnosis still eluding us, we couldn't be sure of what her future would hold or how long that future would extend. Other health issues were threatening: aneurisms, organ failure, palsies. Often, individuals with special needs deal with a host of ailments that arise as they age. Though we didn't dwell on the negative possibilities, we did keep a watch out for trouble. We also evolved into the idea and the practice of going with the moment. Love big and love often.

The day-to-day caregiving kept us busy enough; there wasn't a lot of time for lingering in the disappointments. But to our surprise, it was the little things Hannah did every day that truly grew our appreciation for the Hannah of the "now." We had always loved her and liked her, of course. But we found ourselves profoundly embracing and rejoicing in those everyday things that made her exceptional.

From the age of three, for instance, Hannah could swim. Like me, she felt drawn to water. I loved that. I had enrolled Hannah in swimming lessons at such a young age for the simple fact that we had a pool. If she ever fell in, God forbid, I thought she would at least know how to save herself. She took to it right away. Though her technique is limited to the dog paddle, Hannah can hold her own in water.

Certainly there were plenty of times when "who" Hannah is posed challenges for the family. But isn't that the case with any child? I've mentioned Hannah's stubborn streak. It used to manifest itself in what we called "going Jell-O." If Hannah didn't want to do something, she slowly slumped to the floor and spread out. She was Jell-O. It would take a spatula to get her up.

And another example. When Hannah was a toddler, she made a lot of noises, a common self-stimulating behavior among individuals with certain disabilities. Stimming, as it's sometimes called, is a term used to describe any self-engaging repetitious action or behavior. Rocking, for instance, is another type of stimming behavior, as is clapping, which Hannah did a lot as a toddler. Charlie Jr. was okay with the clapping. But at times her other noises got on his nerves, and mine too. I would tell my son it was all right to feel negatively about such things but that there was nothing we could do about it. I didn't want him to experience guilt for his feelings, but at the same time, he needed to recognize that this was life as we knew it. "We've got to make friends with it," I would tell him. And in time, we all did.

Other aspects of Hannah being Hannah weren't quite so easy to adjust to. Her discomfort in crowds or close quarters, for instance, is still an issue for us. When she experiences a sensory overload, she is likely to have a meltdown. When she was younger, it meant that my mother or the neighbors would sometimes have to take Charlie to his little league games while I stayed home. And of course the large crowds at a football game make those experiences impossible for our daughter.

Today I will still notice a little girl having a blast at a football game and wish it could be Hannah.

Instead, my daughter and I swim in our pool or hit the beach. When we lived in New Jersey, we had a gorgeous pool with an eight-foot deep end. One awesome Indian summer day in October, my brother and his wife came up for a visit, and naturally, Hannah headed for the pool. From the kitchen window, we watched as she, then five, traipsed over to the deep end, stripped off all her clothes, and jumped in. My brother looked like he'd had a heart attack, but I assured him it was okay. "Hannah can swim," I told him. "Naked, but she can swim." It is just one of my daughter's many amazing abilities.

Hannah likes the pool, but she prefers the ocean. She possesses a natural knowledge of the flow of the tide. Intuitively, she knows when the biggest waves are crashing in, when to turn her back, when to let their force lift her up and carry her. A few years ago, when my friend Brenda and I took Hannah to the beach, my friend escorted my daughter out into about three feet of water and left her there. Hannah was farther out than I would have liked, and as Brenda approached me, I was ready to object. Instead, Brenda spoke first. "Look at her," she said. "No one would know that she has special needs right now." And as I gazed at my girl, it was true. There she stood, chest high in that churning life force of ocean water, people splashing all around her. Like them, she was hanging out with the waves.

Charlie and I learned to live on all these moments, the daily accomplishments, the quirky and heartwarming character traits. They fortified us. We lived on them and grew on them. What parents could forget the day their child is potty trained for good, or the first time they hear "I love you"? Imagine, then, the joy that parents experience when their six-year-old takes the first step without stumbling, or the ecstasy of hearing "Mom," or seeing it typed on a tap board, even when the child is much older. For us, we nearly uncorked the champagne when Hannah took to

the potty at seven. And about that first "Love you":
I could never have prepared myself for its power.

Once, when Han was five, she let us know, as
only Hannah could, that she wanted some French
fries. We thought we had understood her but kept
asking her to repeat herself, just to be sure. When
we still weren't positive, we asked her if she could
get what she wanted out of the refrigerator.
Without hesitation, Hannah turned, opened the
freezer, and pulled out a bag of fries. Charlie and I
were ecstatic. Like little kids, we cheered, slapped
high-fives, and jumped up and down. She had
done it! To this day, when Han meets a milestone,
when she pulls out one of her many surprises,
we're like kids caught up in the thrill of the game.

What I learned in the process of discovering
Hannah is that when the wave rolls in, ride it.
Don't anticipate the decline; don't think about
when the next wave will wash in. Another will
come, sometime. Until then, experience the thrill,
feel the rush, ride the joy.

Last year, for instance, another miracle came
sailing in. When Hannah was an infant and a

young toddler, she had this incredible belly laugh, a real barroom gut buster. Later, when her trouble set in, it vanished. For years, I had mourned the loss of that laugh. It fit our jolly girl so appropriately; it was so Hannah. Then one day last fall, Jo—a sweetheart of a young woman who had come to help us with Hannah when she was eight, and whom all of us adore—and I were playing with Hannah and doing all the silly stuff that really gets her tickled. The two of us led off with "Ha, Haaaa . . ." and Hannah lobbed one back at us. Again with "Ha, Haaaa . . ." and Hannah mimicked us again, this time with a smile. Once more, "Ha, Haaaa. . . ." But this time, Hannah's echo trailed on, her laughter dipping and splashing and bubbling like water over rocks, carrying us all away in its resplendence. It was so good to have that laugh back, for however long.

We found laughter in the life we shared with our daughter. Unexpected and unabashed laughter. As parents, we move through our children's stages and phases with them. The good and the bad, the delightful and the disappointing. They are moving ever onward, and we can only tag along. To reach for the next good things with them, we have to let go of some others. Every parent knows the trade-offs. What a thrill to watch the child learn to run, but with that new skill, she bolts right out of the phase in which she let you hold her for hours. And so it goes, receiving and giving over. The rising and the receding of the tide.

We parents store our memories safely, like priceless mementos. And though we may pull them out from time to time, they are never as good as the real thing. Like childhood, their beauty is sweet but fleeting.

Though I've never put away the photo of the Hannah I once knew—it still sits wedged into a corner of my bureau mirror—it is changed for me. What was once a source of motivation, a reminder of the illusory pearl beyond our reach, has become a cherished keepsake of one exquisitely happy moment in our lives. One of many.

From the point of Hannah's early diagnosis, up until she was about eight, we have too few other pictures of her. We have no video recordings documenting those years of her life. It's a regret I'll carry with me always. And not simply because I'd like more snapshots to fill in her scrapbook. The absence of those photos and videos implies that Charlie and I didn't really know all we had in Hannah. Her full beauty eluded us. To me, the hole of those years shows that we were off looking for someone else. We have come to see differently; she had to teach us.

Graciously, miraculously, we found her. Not the girl in the photo. The girl who has our hearts.

CHAPTER 5

MEETING

THE

OUTSIDE

WORLD

I T'S A RAINY DAY IN JUNE, AND CHARLIE, THE kids, and I, along with some close friends, are vacationing in Florida. Do we ever need this! My husband had spent much of the previous year recovering from complications he suffered after surgery. Complications, I say. My husband had slipped into a coma and remained there for two weeks. The doctors had not given him much hope. But even after Charlie had emerged from his near-death experience, he was off his feet for months. He healed, but slowly. Emotionally, it took me longer. That's why this day feels so alive, the break so deserving. We're all together again and celebrating.

But as we head over to Disney World, Hannah pulls at the reins. Clearly, she's not as revved as the rest of us about our outing. But we keep moving with the hope she'll ease into the idea once we arrive. It is an outdoor park, we reason, so maybe she'll feel less confined. Maybe the sheer spectacle of the park itself will blur out the crowds that cause Hannah's discomfort. But as we board the shuttle bus to take us from the hotel to the park, and then as we arrive at the gate and buy our badges, which allow a family with a child who has special needs to move to the front of the ride line, Hannah's tension heightens.

She floats along in the "It's a Small World" ride, not completely comfortable but happier than she's been all day—the music cheering her and carrying her through. It's nice for the moment, but I can see that this won't last.

Later, at another ride, we flash our badges to a ride attendant, who escorts us to the head of the line. All eyes are on us. I know what people are thinking: Where are *they* going? What's wrong with one of them? At seven, Hannah doesn't appear to have any developmental limitations. She walks fine. And she doesn't present any of the physical features that characterize various chronic disabilities. She looks like any other kid.

Then, just before we board the ride, Hannah loses it. She lets loose with her ear-piercing scream and throws herself to the ground. Oh, I'm sure everyone around us is thinking to themselves, *that's* why they were moved to the front of the line. And as Charlie and I plead, order, and bribe to coax our daughter up off the wet ground, I feel the stares burning down on us.

I lift my eyes briefly but long enough to see whole families gawking at Hannah. They can't take their eyes off her, as if she's the main attraction in some freak show. It's not enough that I catch the looks; Hannah does too. She covers her face and cries out as if the bystanders' thoughts pain her. Does she really know what they are thinking, I wonder. Does she feel distraught over her differences, vulnerable, and judged? It's too much for me. Once we get Hannah up, I announce that she and I have had enough and we're leaving. "The people's staring is bothering her and me!" I say loud enough for everyone around us to hear. But Charlie insists that he be the one to return to the hotel with Hannah, and eventually he wins out. They spend the rest of the day at the pool, where Hannah feels more in her element.

The rest of the trip was fine. No outbursts or public scenes. No distraught daughter. But I couldn't regroup and fully enjoy myself. In my eyes, our excursion was shrouded in a cloud cover of unkindness and insensitivity. Even after we returned home, I felt depressed about our experience at the park. It wasn't Hannah's meltdown that bothered me; those happened frequently enough. It was those scornful, aghast, "I'm-glad-it's-not-me" looks our family had been receiving for years. Even after all the time that had passed, all our experiences and growth, those looks still stung like a fresh slap in the face. They still do.

Dealing with external adversity is, to me, the dark side of raising a child who is "different." We knew we would encounter negativity. We expected it. But I, more than Charlie, have had a hard time coming to terms with that fact. Maybe it's because I've borne the brunt of those uncomfortable moments. Maybe it's because of some unnamed or undefined issue buried deep in my psyche. Or perhaps it's because I want to expect the best of people. Whatever the reason, coping with that negativity and formulating a healthy response to it have taken me some time and a lot of work. And because we continue to encounter those instances that incite my anger and disappointment, I keep working on my reaction to them.

Obviously, past experiences still color my present outlook. Like a shooting victim who takes cover when a truck backfires, I have feelings that sometimes lead to rote responses before I've had the chance to think about how I really want to respond. It's posttraumatic stress in the truest sense.

Once, when Hannah was about five, I took her to Charlie Jr.'s Catholic elementary school to see a play in which my son had a role. "These people will be okay," I remember thinking before we went in. But I had not anticipated the size of the crowd. Hannah came apart fifteen minutes before curtain time. Not one person came over to offer help. Not a soul asked if Hannah was all right. Instead, dozens of parents peered over their shoulders and laid their most contemptuous looks on us. Within seconds, they sent us packing. No one had to utter a word. Their faces said it all: "You are not welcome here."

The experience shook me. Here was a whole body of people—probably good people, at least parents who sent their children to religious school—who had scorned us. We had been cast out like lepers, unfit to mingle among their society. If we could not be accepted in *that* circle, I remember thinking, what could we expect of people who had never heard the call to love others as they love themselves?

For weeks after that experience, we stayed close to home. Such cruelty, I had thought. Why would I want to subject Hannah to that ever again? Even now, in certain settings, I still feel the grip of that painful experience, and I have to tell myself not to bolt. That memory and many others stay with me, scars from old wounds.

But as the years have passed, and as I've grown and learned what is best for my daughter, I have gotten more comfortable with stepping out into the world with her. For one, Hannah really likes going out to eat at her favorite restaurant, Applebee's. But I've also moved beyond the idea that I'm denying my daughter many of the good things in life by refusing to take her to places other children might go, only to make her the object of public scrutiny.

I don't want to be misunderstood. I will not put Hannah in any closet. But these days I don't feel the pull to immerse Hannah into different situations simply because they're different or new or they might be "good for her." I've learned that often these experiences aren't good for Hannah, just as it wouldn't be good to give strawberries to a child with a strawberry allergy. Simply put, Hannah does not benefit from experiences that provoke major anxiety in her. They cause her only pain and distress. So, as caring parents, we avoid those situations.

Of course, as any parent of a child with special needs will attest, sometimes you don't have to leave your own home to encounter adversity and prejudice. Visits from close friends and new acquaintances alike have been acutely painful. Too many times I've entered a room to find all eyes on Hannah, as if our guests couldn't help but stare at her. And the looks certainly weren't positive or friendly. To these people, Hannah was a puzzle they couldn't figure out. Sometimes they remind me of people rubbernecking at an auto accident, intrigued by the sheer horror of it.

Even now I'm not sure which offends me more—people staring at my daughter or people pretending not to stare at my daughter. We all know the look: The head is facing away, but the eyes are glued on the kid making the weird noises. It cuts even deeper when you see it happening with members of your own family. I always wonder what they're expecting to see.

One friend's husband was particularly obnoxious. He looked at Hannah as if she were an alien and seemed suspicious of her. I became so sensitive to people's stares that I even developed a mild animosity toward some of Hannah's therapists and doctors. I couldn't stand that they studied her like a lab experiment, deconstructed her like a robot, rather than trying to get to know her as a unique person. They, like so many other people, seemed to see only Hannah's disability, as if it defined her. I've often wondered how anyone could meet her yet miss her charm, her beauty.

Other parents have shared similar stories with me, and we've agreed it's difficult to know which is worse: people continually peering at your child or people not regarding her at all.

The same guy who seemed "afraid" of my daughter also completely ignored her when his child, who was riding a swing, once accidentally kicked Hannah in the face. There sat my girl on the ground, stunned and crying, nose bloodied, while this man easily disregarded her. Instead he ran to his child, who wasn't injured, and comforted her. I was enraged by the mistreatment, by the indifference shown toward my daughter. To him, Hannah was not worthy of notice. She was invisible.

The parents of special needs children, too, withstand critical opinion and undue judgment. Almost every time Hannah has a meltdown in public, at least one person will stare at me like I'm an ax murderer. I want to say to that person, "No, I'm not hurting her, she just does this." I don't, of course. But those looks, especially, get under my skin because I don't believe in physical punishment as a means of enforcement or discipline. Only once did I ever smack Charlie Jr.'s tush, and wisely he responded, "Mommy, I don't hit you. Don't hit me."

We've even been burned by some of our closest friends and family. Once we heard, through the grapevine, that Hannah didn't really suffer from any disability, she was just a spoiled brat. Then I'll never forget the comment from a woman who was airing her opinions about another family's adopted child with noticeable developmental deficiencies. "God knows how many drugs that birth mother was on when she was expecting," she said. I was floored. I hadn't touched a drop of alcohol when I was pregnant with Charlie or Hannah, and I certainly hadn't taken drugs. It horrified me to think that someone might think I had, and even worse, that it might be the prevailing public thinking about parents of children with special needs.

Though we had expected some rough patches, comments and reactions like those I've described caught Charlie and me off-guard. And it wasn't always just the punches that pained us, but also who delivered them. I still carry a wounded heart. But along the way, I've recognized that I care about and love my daughter so much more than I care about what other people think. I look at my girl and think to myself, "You are what matters." My job is to raise my children up in love. How can I do that if others sap my energy or overtake my thoughts? They can interfere, I've decided, only if I allow them to. Taking that consideration to heart, I have made a better effort at casting off negative comments and actions. And to this day, whenever I feel that my daughter and I are under fire, I recite a phrase to myself that my good friend Brenda geared me with years ago: "They don't pay my bills." In other words, I am not indebted to anyone in any way. I owe no explanation for my daughter. While every human being has a place of importance in this world, no one has a place of importance over me, over my daughter, over anyone. In the playing field of life, we all fill the same slot; it's all the same position.

But I'd be lying if I said the stares and the comments no longer hurt. And any parent knows why. It is only because I am consumed with love for her.

Think about it. What parents wouldn't feel a twinge of sorrow for their child if they found him alone on a playground full of children? And who couldn't help but feel heartache after overhearing a critical remark about a child's athletic ability or weight or appearance? When the grenades land, they inflict injury on multiple levels.

Primarily, it pains parents to see such mean-spiritedness directed at their son or daughter. No one deserves such small and careless treatment.

But then we consider how the child must feel, and that's the real source of pain. We worry that the reckless words and the heartless actions will leave an irrevocable mark on that place within the child that is so sensitive and precious. We are the ones who know the marvels of each of our children—the wondrous abilities, the history, the holiness. And we long to tell those who criticize, who brush aside, "If you only knew her." What hurts my child hurts me. It's a parental universal.

Still, other parents seem to disengage from Hannah, which I find so odd, so unnatural. In my case, motherhood had planted an acute sensitivity within me that I had not known before. I was suddenly possessed with the maternal desire for continual closeness with my children and the inclination to protect them from every harm. I felt, for myself, the rev of the internal engine pushing me to do whatever I could for them. And I knew the ache of separation when I had to leave them for the first time. I remember thinking, "So this is what parenthood feels like." Motherhood tinted my view of everything. Everyone was someone's child.

That's why it surprises me when other parents treat my daughter, or any other child or adult with or without special needs, maliciously or insensitively. It escapes me how parents can deny others the kindness and understanding they would want bestowed on their own children. They don't have to know my daughter the way I do; they couldn't possibly. But how well we know each other shouldn't matter, I believe. As humans joined together by a common place and time, bound together and born of the same source, we all deserve respect and mercy.

Perhaps one of the most hurtful experiences with Hannah happened when she was four years old. She and I had headed out in the car to pick up Charlie Jr. from school. It was a cloudy, late spring day, and the sky had let loose with a steady downpour. When we arrived at the school, I grabbed Hannah up in my arms, threw up the umbrella, and the two of us made a dash for the doors. The wind whipped about, and rain soaked our feet, hands, and faces. When we entered the school, we were both breathless, smiling, and giggling. What an adventure we'd had! And what a priceless moment for both of us. There we were, caught up in the wind and the rain and each other. Just Hannah and Mommy.

Then, while one-handedly collapsing the umbrella, I noticed a woman standing near us talking on the phone. We had not been loud, not loud enough to disturb her conversation. Yet this woman glared at us, at Hannah, with a look of utter disdain. It was a look people often threw at my daughter, who at the time had a large tummy and was big for her age. The look of the woman told me she was disgusted by the sight of her.

My heart dropped into my stomach. And as we made our way down the hall, I turned to see the woman craning her head around the corner, keeping us in the hold of her hurtful gaze. It was early yet in our discovery of Hannah's condition, and I was edgier than usual. With my anger percolating within me, I shot off, "What are you staring at?! She is a baby! She is a child!"

I've often wondered why that woman had to be there then. Why that instant, when we were so sweetly lost in our own world? Why that look, which pierced our special moment? And the only answer I've been able to come up with is this: so that I could learn early on the devastation that can be wielded with one insensitive stare.

These days, whenever Hannah and I encounter insensitivity or unkindness, I'm slower to respond with words. Instead, I deliver my own look, which I hope conveys to people to watch their step and that they can't tread on me or my daughter. If that doesn't work, then I do say a few words. It's my obligation, I believe, to set people straight; I don't think God minds if I challenge their convictions. As Hannah's mother, it's part of my role to defend her. She has no voice, so I must use mine.

In some respects, I may really sound like an ax murderer, ready to pounce on my next victim. But airing my grievances is not my intention or my goal. I share these stories, in part, because I really do have faith in humankind. First, I trust that many people do not recognize the hurt they cause by their actions or, in some cases, inaction. For some reason, it just doesn't occur to them. But I also believe that when people are made aware of their harmful tendencies or wrongdoings—intentional or unintentional—they are inclined to change their ways.

Often it does take a dramatic incident to clear our view—an unforgettable exchange or experience that shakes up preconceived notions and allows us to see the world from a new vantage point. That day of arriving at the school in the rain was only one of many life-altering lessons. Maybe something I've shared here will provide a similar lesson for someone else.

Perhaps these examples will help people recognize the pain that many parents of children with special needs endure. Perhaps they will heighten sensitivity toward people with differences. Maybe they will give people pause and encourage them to conscientiously and conscionably respond to individuals with special needs and their families in ways that are supportive, accepting, uplifting. If that can happen, who knows how we can all benefit?

And so I claim a broader purpose for my personal revelations. The crimes against Hannah, against me, are not simply against Hannah or me. Fundamentally, I believe, they are wrongs against all of humanity and transgressions against God and the larger good.

Today's world can be so intolerant, impatient, and immovable. But if we cannot overlook the most minor irritants and the slightest differences, what have we become as a civilization, as humans derived from the divine? Only by internalizing the situations of others and acknowledging them with consideration and understanding can we demonstrate goodwill and a generous spirit toward all people. Only then, I believe, can we recognize our fullest life, our highest calling.

There's a tendency—some might call it a defense mechanism—after encountering so much hurt and negativity to turn the gaze of judgment around. The one searching for mercy assumes the eye of condemnation. I have seen through that lens at times, and all is tainted. In time, though, with growth, with patience, with endless prayer

and a seeking heart, I have learned to be more forgiving. It's a discipline, a decision to circle back
and see the world with a loving, forgiving heart.

I know that the stories I've shared may fright-
en some parents newly discovering their child's
"differences." Don't let them. Rather, think about
how you will respond to the harshness you will
likely encounter. Start now, and with thoughtful
consideration, prayer, and introspection, decide
the type of parent, the type of person, you want to
be. Will you be a person who upon receiving negativity sends it flying back? Will you more passive-
ly accept negativity because of a prevailing doubt
that things will ever be different? Or will you be
the kind of parent who, recognizing the essential
beauty of your child, chooses to work and pray
for a world of change? I choose to hope, to pray,
to change.

A small part of me was reluctant to move back
to New Jersey with Hannah when we did. We had
a history there, people knew Charlie and me even
before we were married. Initially, when we
returned, we became the subjects of pity by some.

We didn't deserve pity. I resented that people felt sorry for us, especially when they did not know our entire story, and certainly not our daughter.

One woman was so bold as to tell me that Hannah was my cross to bear. I was stunned. Hannah was my daughter, not my burden. I was not worthy of admiration for "carrying" her through life. I had not been afflicted, I had been blessed.

To me, true compassion means attempting to understand someone's difficult situation and to refrain from casting judgment on it. Compassion is feeling for people without feeling sorry for them. It's extending a warm heart toward people who are in the midst of hard times. As we reach further toward understanding one another, compassion becomes easier to grasp, for we recognize more clearly the commonality among us all.

So the next time you see a mother or a father engaged with a child with special needs, offer a kind word, provide a hand, share a simple smile. Not surprisingly, of all the people who felt sorry for us, not one ever offered us help. True compassion doesn't just move the soul, it compels us to action.

When Hannah was about five, she used to run out of the house. There didn't have to be a reason; sometimes she'd just see the door and decide to leave. Though we'd secure the house, sometimes she still figured out how to work the front lock.

One of those times, I searched all over the house for her and couldn't find her. I was home alone, and I knew she was gone. I ran out into the yard, but she wasn't there either. I saw a neighbor and screamed to her that Hannah was missing.

I don't have to describe the wrenching thoughts that seized my mind at that moment. I raced through the neighborhood, looking in desperation for my daughter. When I couldn't find her, I rushed home to call the police. How I hated to pick up that phone, to have to make that dreaded call. In a way, it felt as though I was fixing Hannah's fate. But just then, I heard my neighbor Ruth calling from next door. "I've got her! She's here! She's on my swing set!"

It would not be the only time Hannah gave us such a scare. She left the house one night when Charlie Jr. and I were home together. We found her in our backyard, sitting in a trench for our new septic system.

I am eternally grateful to Ruth, the neighbor who did not judge me when she found my daughter. She had been focused solely on finding Hannah. I was in need, and Hannah was in need. That was enough. Ruth was with us, swept up in the current of compassion that flows within every human being, just beneath the surface.

When we moved from New Jersey, I would find my daughter asleep with a photo of her former classmates and teachers clutched to her chest. She would fall asleep crying because she missed them. With everyone, Hannah longs to make herself known and loved. Sadly, so many people Hannah encounters live with limitations— a narrow mind, a cloistered heart. I long to let them in on the secret, to say to them, "If you only knew her."

I've discovered in recent years that my daughter does know of her differences. There are times, just out of the blue, when Hannah will look at me mournfully and say, "I'm sorry." She means, "I'm sorry I'm like this. I'm sorry this is hard on you. I'm sorry for your hurt." That is exactly what she means, and it breaks my heart.

Those words come so easily from my girl, from a child with a limited vocabulary, from a person whom so many people readily discount. But it is also she who feels my hurt, who appreciates my vulnerability, who recognizes my human fragility. Just two words. And she is not the one who needs to say them. "God gave me the perfect girl in you, Hannah," I tell her. "I love you, and you are perfect."

At times, when the thought of undergoing yet another test of the world brings on an anticipatory wince from me, I turn my thoughts to Hannah. She, like so many other children and adults with special needs, has to work so much harder than I do just to accomplish what is considered "normal" to the rest of us. She struggles just to get through life, and yet she makes the best of it as she carries her disability with her every day. She is my hero.

From the beginning, such a brave little soul: putting her faith in me, trusting that I knew what was right. When, really, I was learning too.

Each day that dawns, Hannah is there, greeting it with open arms. She welcomes the world at its best and at its worst. And so must I. I pray for strength, knowing I have my daughter to live up to.

CHAPTER 6

Seeking the Spirit

ODAY HANNAH IS ONE DAY OLD, AND HER visitor is a Catholic nun. The woman is here, in the hospital, to perform Hannah's baptism. After some words to us and the baptismal liturgy, Sister gently marks the sign of the cross on Hannah's forehead: a sign of acknowledgment that Hannah is bound to God in this life and the life after.

Though Hannah's birth was free of complications, she is not. Because of the condition of her kidneys, the thread to which she clings to life is tenuous, we've been told. It was in our best interest to be prepared. So we called in the nun for the urgent baptism. Though her baptism at the hospital comforts us, it is a solemn affair. We rejoice in the gift of Hannah, always knowing she belongs to God first. Yet we can't help but want more of her.

When Hannah is released from the hospital after a mere three-day stay, throwing a party feels like the only thing to do. She is God's, a miraculous child shared with us, and we want to share our gift with all the world.

We celebrate another baptism with Hannah, this one officiated by a priest from a local parish where the parishioners prayed for our family daily during the last two months of my pregnancy. It just couldn't feel more right to me. This place, these people, our family embraced in prayer.

After the ceremony, we invite all our family and closest friends to the stadium club for the celebration of Hannah's life and our life together. It's a spectacular day, with music and laughter and Hannah asleep in my arms. Throughout the entire day, she sleeps, waking only to eat. She is at ease, and so am I. Holding her gives me calm, brings me peace. Hannah's godmother comes over and strokes my daughter's head. "I think she's going to be a nun," she says. "There's just something spiritual about Hannah."

⁄ℴ

While I trust that there is indeed a spiritual side to all humankind and all living beings, there was no denying, as Hannah grew up, the specific holiness of her being. Apart from her gentle temperament, Hannah embodied something more, something mysterious. So many times I would look at her and feel as if I was regarding more than the person in front of me. To me, she seemed to hold a divine secret. And as I would watch her sleep, I felt I was in the presence of an angel.

I wasn't alone with my thoughts and feelings; Charlie and others sensed something different about Hannah too. Whenever we enrolled Hannah in a new school or paired her with new therapists, we would initially encounter looks of skepticism from Hannah's instructors. They were sure she would be tough to handle, problematic, unreachable. But after spending one week with our daughter, Hannah's teachers and therapists would find themselves completely taken with her, surprised at her abilities and attitude, and charmed by her ways. Excitedly, they would share with us story after story of what Hannah had done on any particular day. Our daughter would win them over with ease. And Charlie and I would smile at each other and say she had worked her "Hannah magic" once again.

But only as the years progressed, as our grief subsided into the past, and as we grew to adore our girl for precisely who she is, did we recognize Hannah's true connection with the world around her. Like someone introduced to the inner workings of a clock, or the explorer who sets eyes on a snowcapped mountain range for the first time, we watched in wonder as another dimension of our daughter emerged into our view.

～

It's a stunning summer day, and Hannah is in the backyard. I find her where I usually do, in front of the bed that is bursting with flowers in bright full bloom. Among them are the black-eyed Susans, beaming as the sun. I watch as Hannah sits herself down, immersing herself in them. She stares and stares. But her face doesn't bear the faraway look of a girl lost in a distant dream. Her eyes are fixed on each petal, every stem, admiring the colors and the textures, the contours and the lines. She is so still, so focused. After a while, it becomes clear to me that she is no longer looking, but listening, absorbed in the lyrical forces of life, hearkening to a universal rhythm. The world's distinctions dissolve, and she is no longer separate from it.

❧

My daughter's spiritual makeup, as well as her spiritual life, is abundantly visible to me. I'm sure I "see" these facets of her, in part, because I expect to. My receptors are open; the signals have a way in. It is similar to the way I am expectant of and receptive to God's workings in my life. God is always present, I believe, as are the effects of God. Whether or not we are attuned to that presence and those effects depends a great deal on us. If we keep the shades drawn, much will be missed.

I am certain Hannah is in relation with the divine. As created individuals, I believe, we all possess that potential. I do not need to hear Hannah's prayers or see her immersed in scriptures or receiving the sacraments to believe she shares a relationship with God. Our true communion with the Creator, it seems to me, is mostly unseen. It takes place deep within our souls.

And yet I feel there have been many times when I have witnessed my daughter's experiences of at-oneness with the universe or happened upon her in a moment of spiritual intimacy. Appreciating the exquisite beauty of flowers, the calming motion of riding her swing, the feel of sand on her feet, the crashing of waves, the weightlessness of her body in water, the kindness in her grandmother's face. All moments of holy communion. For Hannah, these are very real encounters with the divine. I've learned they are not limited to the grand and the spectacular. They are revealed, too, in the simplest things.

❦

Hannah is seven years old and still in diapers. Many individuals with special needs have to wear diapers for a lifetime. That's not so unusual. But Hannah, we think, is capable of using the potty. She has nothing that hinders her physically from doing so. Still, it could be that she will never use it.

Though we are prepared for that possibility, we had attempted to train her ourselves. When that didn't happen, we took a break and picked up with it again at another time. And when that try was also unsuccessful, we decided to go for another round later. Then we called in help.

We'd heard about the Groden Center in Providence, Rhode Island, which, among other things, offers home services for special needs families. When Hannah was five, Maryanne, the supervisor of the center's home-based services, began meeting with us four days a week after school. She stayed for three hours a day and spent the entire time working with Hannah on the particulars of potty usage. Two years later, Hannah was still in diapers.

That's when Maryanne tried convincing us she needed a weekend alone with Hannah. Charlie and I weren't sure. Leave our girl at home with someone else? But after two years, Maryanne was practically family. We trusted her, so we gave her suggestion a go.

Now, returning home, we don't know what to expect. Will Hannah be diaper free? Will we find Maryanne sobbing in a corner, defeated? Or will the two of them be camped out on the bathroom floor?

But as we come through the door, everything is in its typical order. There's no crying or screaming. Hannah is happy to see us, and Maryanne is calm and smiling. We're all visiting when Hannah walks away from us. She's headed for the bathroom, and we notice a look in her eyes. She is so pleased with herself. Her face tells it all: "Mom and Dad, prepare to be wowed."

∽

I think it's fair to say I did not fully appreciate God in the minor movements of life. Preparing meals, organizing schedules, and washing clothes and dishes were nothing more than the mundane tasks that filled my life.

But as I watched Hannah grow and develop, those duties took on a new significance for me. What I considered to be easy, mindless tasks were challenging feats for my daughter. Accomplishing even the simplest actions—holding a pencil, feeding herself with her hands, nudging a ball with her foot—brought her such pleasure and satisfaction. And yet, those were actions I took for granted every day.

And I came to this realization: Every aspect of our lives, every experience, thought, and action, from the profound to the mundane, exists within God. Every day we are immersed in the sacred. Nothing we do is beyond it. And so, I believe, every moment of life, every action in it, is an opportunity for awe and thanksgiving.

That is why we cheer our daughter when she completes a task she's done a thousand times before. Why I try not to grumble over the cutting board while I'm cooking dinner. Why we take the opportunity to tell our kids we love them, even in front of their friends. If I am truly living in God, what else can I do?

Though there will always be things I don't want and don't like to do, no amount of complaining will improve them or make them go away. (Anyway, shouldn't I be glad I can do them at all?) Besides, if my daughter can face the situations of her life that cause her discomfort, even trauma, then who am I to complain about the inconvenient and the uninspiring? I don't hear Hannah bemoan her situation or her limitations, even though I know they frustrate her. She's happy being able to use the potty.

∽

It's dinner-out night, and Jo, our nanny, is Hannah's companion at Applebee's. It's early, before the big crowds arrive. And Hannah is comfortable, talking with Jo, looking around. The two share grins and recall the highlights of the day in an easy and caring exchange.

At the end of the meal, a waitress, maybe all of seventeen, stops at the table. "You are so great with her. I wish I could learn to be like that," she tells Jo. "She is so awesome, she brings a smile to my face just by looking at her."

∽

I hope we have all encountered people in our lives with whom we connect in ways that go beyond the physical. Though we interact verbally with these individuals, we exchange more than words. It's as if our souls are also conversing, responding to what is familiar in the other. The realization of a common source, true contact. It can't be manufactured.

On the same level, I believe, it's Hannah's spiritual nature and her connection to the overarching forces of life that afford her entry into so many people's lives and hearts. People are simply drawn to her, even complete strangers from across a restaurant. I don't think this attraction is due to anything she does as much as who she is. The light of her spirit pulls people in.

Similarly, I believe, Hannah recognizes and responds to the spiritual essence of others. I base this on Hannah's ability to discriminate between those who support her and those who do not. She picks up on the positive and negative energies that others display toward her. And she can read people for who they are. When a longtime friend of mine fell into a morally compromising lifestyle, Hannah sensed that something in that person had changed. I never told Hannah what I knew. But Hannah was clearly repelled by what she saw and is still reluctant to be around this person today.

It is true that given the characteristics of her disability, Hannah does balk at most new encounters with people. You have to put in time with Hannah before she can feel comfortable and open up to you. But when she absolutely refuses to warm up to someone, it's a cue to us: this person is not a fit for our daughter or for us right now.

More remarkably, though, Hannah's highly defined view of the spirit puts her in touch with others' pain. She senses people's loneliness, their grief, and their fear. She peers, as through a window, into the heart of the individual.

∽

It's Hannah's first day at her new school and she enters the classroom with her aid, Kathy. This is a huge transition for Hannah—the different setting, all the unfamiliar faces. She is scared and nervous and asks to go home. Then another female aid walks through the door.

Hannah takes one look at her and crosses the room, moving past people and toys toward the woman, who is standing alone. The two have never met, yet Hannah wraps arms with her and clutches her hands.

The aid is stunned, a little taken aback. She had entered the room cautiously too; she is also afraid and unsure. And yet a little girl she has never met clings to her.

There is no way Hannah could have known about this woman, about her loss, that a fifteen-year-old girl she had cared for since preschool had died just months earlier. Yet, somehow, Hannah *does* seem to know, and she is drawn to the place in this woman that needs reassurance, comfort, and healing.

The woman decides to stay just for the day. And she returns the next day and the day after that. She comes because of Hannah, because of the incredible bond they share and the hope Hannah brings her.

One day Kathy sees the woman holding Hannah in a tearful embrace. "I get such a warm feeling from her," she tells Kathy. "It's as if my little friend is right here with me."

ᴄ∕ᴐ

The skeptics would say that these stories prove nothing. They might argue that these experiences do not reveal, for absolute certain, that Hannah perceives the supernatural, that she interacts with these forces, or even that a spiritual nature subsists in her being. And I would agree. They don't *prove* anything.

But there is no denying that these experiences happened, that through an encounter with Hannah, someone came away with a new outlook on life, or another felt less apprehensive or hurt. There is no denying the very real effects she has had on the lives of others, or the remarkable suitability of those who have come to have an impact on hers. Connections have been made.

But those connections are tough to pin down. They don't stand out like gold stars on school papers. They don't help us gauge where we stand in comparison to others.

In our achievement-oriented culture, we don't pay much attention to what we can't measure. Instead, we tend to stick to what we can calculate or what's comfortable, what we know. And we know the principle of work and reward. We follow the stocks to balloon our financial portfolios, we educate ourselves to get a better foothold in the job market, we study tape and strategize plays to ensure more wins. But when our lives are only about identifying goals and charting progress, it seems to me we lose touch with the important stuff that can't be counted or sized up.

Certainly, there is nothing wrong with securing one's retirement or earning a doctorate degree or scaling the ranks in one's profession. But the sum of who we are isn't based on our achievements and contributions. Our worth, I believe, rests in our intrinsic value, which originates in the self and hinges on nothing else. We cannot earn it or lose it; it is not contingent on age or ethnicity, race or gender, or IQ. It's the seed buried deep within each of us, identifying us as equals and unique and parts of the whole.

If we live by the measuring stick of accomplishment, I believe, we suffer a sad disconnect from those aspects of our beings that are limitless.

We also run the serious danger of devaluing opportunities, experiences, and people who don't conform to the standard of that measurable scale. And for good reason, that concerns me.

My daughter, I'm told, is globally developmentally delayed. She will never know the sum of two plus two. Unlike my son, she was not reading at age three. She'll never read. In fact, she won't reach many of the benchmarks associated with "normal" childhood development. For us, like many other parents of children with special needs, the notion of "what to expect" when your child is one or two or twelve has lost relevance and meaning.

Instead, we've come to recognize that Hannah resides in a realm that is different from ours. Her soul is at one and at work with the universal spirit. And her heart dwells in what is unseen.

❧

We haven't known Hannah's new aid, Kathy, long, but it's clear to us that she's suited for Hannah and for our family. Kathy feels the same,

she tells us. According to her, the providence of
her life tells her she's right where she's supposed
to be.

Her story begins with her mother's struggle
with Alzheimer's. Kathy, a teacher for more than
twenty years, took a sabbatical from work to help
care for her. In the months before she died, the
mother's dementia worsened, and Kathy was sure
her mom experienced hallucinations. "She would
talk about seeing a little girl in the house," Kathy
tells us. The mother was so bothered by the fact
that Kathy couldn't see the girl that she described
her to Kathy, telling of her long dark hair and
blue eyes.

Kathy's mother deteriorated quickly, and her
sickness deeply affected her speech. But the day
before her mother's death, Kathy recalls, her
mother was remarkably lucid.

"I need for you to know that I'm heaven
bound," the mother said. Kathy replied that she
was sure of that. "No, now," her mother added.
"They're here." It was her husband, her mother,
and a close friend. Then she pointed to the place

in front of the window where she always saw the little girl. "She's going to stay here with you, and she's going to take care of you," the dying woman told her daughter. "Don't worry. You *are* going to see her, and you're really going to love her."

A month later, we introduced Kathy to our black-haired, blue-eyed Hannah.

❧

Just recently I had to take Hannah to have blood drawn for a series of tests. Make no mistake, Hannah is no fan of anything medical. Like most kids, she has learned to associate a visit to the clinic or the doctor's office with the poke of a needle. In Hannah's case, though, it isn't just the threat of pain but other factors, too, that cause her anxiety and discomfort.

So as I pulled into the office parking lot, Hannah dug in her heels. She wasn't going in, she told me in not so many words. I got out of the truck, walked over to her side, and opened the door. "Hannah," I said, "Let's just do this. Let's get it done. Real quick. Real easy."

Without another objection, Hannah popped out of her seat. We strolled into the office, where a nurse was waiting for us, and kept right on going into the procedure room. Hannah settled onto the table and stuck out her arm. A few minutes later, it was over. As we headed back to the truck, Hannah looked at me and said, "Easy."

But I know better. Walking into that office was *not* easy for Hannah. But then, most of life isn't. And I wonder if she ever wishes she had chosen differently. Yes, that's right. After all these years with Hannah, I have come to believe she is here, as she is, willingly. She came into this life, I think, knowing what would be waiting for her.

In the course of raising Hannah, I've experienced so many moments of new understanding and grace that I consider her my divine gift. To me, she is truly an angel come to live among us. It's a belief I hold about all individuals with special needs. I have met too many of them, gotten to know too many parents who share our same story, heard from too many people who relate their incredible experiences with special needs persons, to think anything else.

You only have to spend time with persons with special needs, I believe, to recognize all they offer, all they bring us. To me, they are teachers, instructing us how to live. They are guides, showing us where to seek and find the profound. They are healers, working to set us right again. They are messengers, revealing glimmers of who we really are and what awaits us when we finally arrive at a place of truth.

That's why I think of Hannah and others who are like her as angels. God entrusted Hannah to our care and called her to fill *our* special needs. And as she and others show us how to exist with purpose, they also lead us to discover the very purpose of our existence.

∽

Taped to my computer monitor are photos of children I've come to know through the Hannah & Friends Foundation. Their parents write or e-mail me and send along snapshots. Every day that I sit down to work, I'm greeted by their faces, most of them smiling, awash in the glow from the computer screen.

I have mere fragments of their stories, yet I feel I know these children well. Like Hannah, they are among the "set apart." And like Hannah, I believe, they possess a view of the otherworldly that escapes the rest of us. The God they know up close and personal, we get in mere glimpses. And while we search for clarity of the divine, it is present among them.

I carry the faces of these children in my mind as I attend a meeting about our planned development of group homes for individuals with special needs. The room is full of neighbors who live around the parcel of land where we'd like to break ground. They are curious, and we are here to answer their questions and discuss their concerns about the proposed development. We touch on building design, living capacity, traffic patterns. Then someone asks me, "What are the people like who will live in the community?"

I answer what my heart tells me is true, that they are some of the kindest and purest people on this planet. And that their neighbors needn't worry about their doing drugs, drinking, or partying. "But," I add, "they might want to help clean your yard or do a job for you. And when they see you, they will always wave and say, 'Hi.'"

∽

My daughter has but a few basic needs. Beyond food, clothing, and shelter, she also requires love and companionship. And as I've raised her, I've discovered that these are my basic needs too. In fact, love and companionship are what we all need. Still, it's very easy to find ourselves mostly preoccupied with all the other stuff of life. We get caught up in the distractions and diversions that steer us away from center. And we forget sometimes to be thankful for all we've been given, for necessities met.

I'm sure people wonder if having a child with special needs would be a deal breaker for them and their marriage. When you add up all the unrealized hopes and expectations, all the concerns about health, development, and education, all the daily caregiving that can come with a child who has special needs, it might seem that true gratitude would be tough to muster. That giving thanks for love when a child doesn't communicate or has to endure round after round of surgery would be impossible.

Yet for our family, just the opposite happened. Certainly, we've felt the heartache. We have struggles. But these only help us see why we are here. Because of Hannah, I have come to recognize that we are not obligated to give thanks but that we are designed to. We are prone to it. It is our virtue; it forms the rightness of our being.

And I know now that the path of love is laid out beneath my feet. It is where I started and where I'm destined to go. My daughter walks before me, and it's her light I follow.

A Place

of

Our Own

"YOU KNOW WHAT, HANNAH?" I USED TO SAY TO my daughter, "When you're a teenager, then we'll talk." I had once thought that given enough time, enough therapy, maybe a breakthrough on her true diagnosis and new medical treatments, that just maybe it could happen. It seemed wrong to expect any less.

Now, heading back from a neurologist in Chicago, it seems we have the answer we've been after all these years. Hannah, we've come to learn, has ESES, Electrical Status Epilecticus during Sleep, or Tassinaris syndrome. In short, she has a very specific and rare kind of epileptic seizure disorder. Her history matches the clinical description almost precisely. Normal development through the mid- to late-toddler years, and then the sudden appearance of autistic-like characteristics. Deteriorating motor functions, the cessation of speech, wakefulness due to night seizures. That's our Hannah all right.

Still, I can't help but feel hesitant. Hannah has been misdiagnosed so many times. And so often I suffered the disappointment when "the answer" just within our reach didn't pan out. If we knew what she had, what had happened to her, I once believed, then maybe we could find something to help her. Maybe we could make her life just a little bit easier. But so far, nothing. So even though this new theory seems viable, we decide to send the report to another neurologist, just to be sure.

Within days, we hear back. The neurologist confirms this new diagnosis, and just like that our search now seems over. This is it.

With the proper medications, we're told, we can control our daughter's seizures. Of course, getting the right medication in the right dosage at the right time (age is a variable) will require some tinkering. But essentially, that's all we need to do. To our profound relief, the syndrome does not progress, nor is it typically followed by other health complications. Basically, Hannah's condition will not worsen.

But there's a bonus, we learn. Hannah's seizures likely will cease when she reaches her mid-teens. And at that point, the doctors and literature tell us, individuals with the syndrome generally see an improvement in mental retardation, psychiatric disturbances, and, yes, language dysfunction. Although the outcomes are varied and differ from individual to individual, it seems there just might be a chance that my teenage daughter and I will have our talks.

My heart swells with the possibility, but I know to temper my enthusiasm. In life, I've learned, there are no guarantees. Instead, I feel grateful for the reassurances about Hannah's health and pleased that her communication skills may improve. But, oddly, I'm not as elated about discovering Hannah's diagnosis as I thought I'd be. Surprisingly to me, this is no Super Bowl moment.

Here we've been searching all this time, looking for the key that would help us unlock the mystery of our daughter. And now we have it. Finally, certain fears are put to rest, specific worries quieted. At last I can set aside some lingering suspicions and doubts. And I know now that we *can* provide Hannah with what she needs to help her experience a joyful, fulfilling life.

Yet, though I'm glad for the news, it feels more like a ripple than the tidal wave I had anticipated. But when I think about it, the happenings of life do strike me differently now than they did during those excruciating early days when Hannah's trouble first emerged, or during the years after with all their upheaval and change. Somewhere along the line, I've grown accustomed to this existence, to its uncertainty, and to Hannah as she is. I am at peace and happy.

For so many years, I thought I could find these things only on the *other* side of the door. That *when* we had our answer about Hannah, *then* we could realize a full and joyous and satisfied life. What I failed to see back then were all the other doors that were open to me. I had not noticed them at all until Hannah led me through them, until I found myself dazzled by the light of day.

Happiness is here. It's right here. It's with me. And I know now that whether Hannah and I have

our all-night girl sessions or not, it's all right.
We've had the bad, the good, and here we are.
Whatever happens, whatever Hannah's future
holds, I can *live* with it. And I don't just mean
accept it. I mean I can embrace it, cherish it, and
give thanks for every blessed moment of it.

I hope others can look at where they are standing in their journey of raising a child with special
needs and say to themselves, "We've come this far.
Here we are. This is tough, but we're doing it,
together."

Happiness is here. And here is where we are.

⁓

As Hannah ages, I see a lovely, social side of
her emerging. It's nice, I won't deny it. When my
son, Charlie, has his friends over to the house,
Hannah is right there in the thick of things. She
squeezes in on the couch and enjoys the conversation and the attention she gets, from the girls
mostly. Sharon, the executive director of Hannah
& Friends, jokes that Hannah is young Charlie's
"chick magnet."

That may or may not be true, but one thing is for certain: Charlie watches to see how people treat his sister. He pays attention to the words people use, to how they act when they are around her. He is her ally, her loyal protector. But in a way, she watches out for him, too, I believe. Had it not been for Hannah, I'm not sure Charlie would have developed such a strong moral conscience or would be as mindful of others as he is. He is a loving young man; that is his nature. But I have to think that having Hannah as his sister has helped shape him into a person who embraces people's differences and who recognizes the importance of extending love to everyone. Would he have come to realize these lessons so keenly if not for Hannah? It's a question I also ask of myself.

At times, I think of myself as a young tree with many rings. My daughter has aged me, and that's a good thing. I consider sometimes all I would have missed had there been no Hannah. Would I have come to my realizations with time, with age and experience? Or would it all have been lost? When I think of my life journey with Hannah and my role as her mother, I cannot help but stand in humility. Because somehow, inexplicably, it is she who has raised me up.

We hear that, don't we? That really, as we instruct and protect our children, as we orchestrate their lives, we the parents are the pupils. We're the ones being worked on. Sometimes the lessons we learn hit us squarely. Mostly, though, they arrive so discreetly that it is only as we are looking over a shoulder, trying to catch a glimpse of what our children are doing now, where they have gone, that we notice the fine particulates that have settled on us and in us. They make up our breath, form our substance. And in their coming together, we find ourselves transformed.

Where we are now, it feels like we are nestling into the place where we are meant to be. Charlie is getting the best of both worlds, living out his dream job at Notre Dame and living out his life *with* his family. He and I and the kids are loving this newfound time together. Also, young Charlie and Hannah are comfortable, attending good schools and finding fast friendships. And I know that a divine hand has led us here; what to find, or learn, or give, we'll have to see.

If anything, life with Hannah has been unexpected. I did not know I could live with such suffocating fear or survive such drowning sorrow. Nor did I know that merely talking to someone could move me into a place of safety, to a higher ground where I could see my situation and my daughter differently. I had no idea that our family could bind so strongly together or that a simple kind gesture could move me to the depths of my being. I did not fully know the healing touch of creation, the inseparable intimacy of God, the sustaining and liberating power of love. And still, I am learning and ready for all that awaits me.

Hardships aren't tests of God, I believe, they are a fact of life. No life is without pain or struggle or suffering. And I think it's for good reason. Without them, would we ever be compelled to call up the best parts of ourselves or to seek the grand essentials of life? Who can say? But we do know that from the adverse and the painful, it is possible to draw out that which is most excellent: compassion, peace, love, forgiveness. Sometimes even, we are left holding these treasures despite ourselves. So I am thankful for the good and the bad, for grace and refinement.

The therapist I visited years ago once told me that life is like an unfinished tapestry. It's a work in progress. When we're in the middle of it, our view is limited. The work seems messy, misshapen, frayed. But when we regard the finished creation, then we will know the completeness of its beauty.

ACKNOWLEDGMENTS

I GRATEFULLY THANK THE FOLKS AT AVE MARIA Press who approached me with the idea of publishing our family's story. It was something I had considered, in an offhand sort of way, for many years but always filed away in the category of "someday." The encouragement and attentive support of the publisher, Tom Grady, as well as Mike Amodei, Mary Andrews, Keri Suarez, and Kathy Coleman, brought this work forward while also assuring us we were in good hands. I'm also thankful to Jessica Trobaugh Temple for her part in this book. She is the one person who could relay our spiritual journey and get it right. Of all the teachers and therapists we've encountered, we are indebted to a few in particular. Amy, Hannah's first teacher in the early-intervention program in Wall Township, New Jersey, went the extra mile for Hannah and for us. And Kelly, one of Hannah's teachers in Cumberland, Rhode Island, is the best special education teacher we've ever met. Our thanks to the Groden Center in Providence, Rhode Island, and specifically to Mare, who coordinated Hannah's services and whom we came to regard as another member of our family. Then there are the aids who have touched Hannah's life, Terri and Kathy, who have been like second mothers to her. When Hannah was nine, Jo entered our lives and relieved me of my Barney duties. She is Hannah's best friend, and because of her, Charlie Jr. has his life back. My thanks to Brenda, who has been a great emotional support to me for many years. And to my mother, the only person who was always there for me, for Hannah, and for Charlie Jr. We would not be where we are today if it were not for her love and care, which she gave selflessly. I thank my son, Charlie Jr., for his understanding, his smile. And I'm grateful to Charlie for being the best husband a woman could ever have. His love for his family is unconditional. To the families of individuals with different abilities, we are all blessed with our gifts from God. May God give us the wisdom to see our gifts and share our stories. My gratitude goes out to all individuals with special needs. As God's ambassadors, they have much to show and teach the world throughout their lives. May they be cherished always.

MAURA WEIS

TO TOM GRADY AND AVE MARIA PRESS, THANK YOU FOR allowing me the opportunity to be a part of this work and for the thoughtful guidance all along the way. To my husband, Kerry, for his many reassurances and loving support. My gratitude goes out to him, my family, and the baby sitters for the generous gift of their time. And for extending their trust to me, I graciously thank the Weises. Maura, thank you for welcoming me into the circle of your family and for bravely sharing your story.

JESSICA TROBAUGH TEMPLE

ABOUT

HANNAH

& FRIENDS

H|ANNAH & FRIENDS, INITIATED IN 2003, SEEKS to foster compassion for the special needs community by also raising public awareness of it. Through the foundation's website, www.hannahandfriends.org, Charlie and Maura Weis share their story of raising their special needs daughter, Hannah, while offering a place for other families to come and relate, to seek and question.

Acknowledging the day-to-day challenges of individuals with special needs and their families, the foundation also funds a grant program called Hannah's Helping Hands. The program offers $100 to $500 grants to qualified Indiana and Rhode Island families and caregivers. In the near future, the foundation will also open a community development that will eventually feature sixteen group homes for special needs individuals who are eighteen and older. Residents will have the opportunity to help operate a farm on the property's thirty acres in South Bend, Indiana, while getting to know the surrounding community. Individuals interested in donating to the foundation or seeking grant assistance can refer to the website or correspond by mail to:

Hannah & Friends

P.O. Box 1218

Granger, IN 46530

Maura Weis is the co-founder of Hannah & Friends, which she and her husband Charlie Weis, head football coach at the University of Notre Dame, started in 2003 in order to honor their daughter Hannah and all people with special needs. Maura was born in Manhattan and lived on the east coast for many years before moving to Notre Dame. She and Charlie have two children, Charlie Jr. and Hannah. In addition to her dedicated and tireless work on behalf of spreading the message of awareness and compassion for people with special needs, she is an accomplished horsewoman and animal lover. Maura and Charlie's dream is to fund and build a farm for young adults with special needs in the South Bend area.

Jessica Trobaugh Temple is a 1992 graduate of the University of Notre Dame and a lifelong resident of South Bend, Indiana. She won three journalism awards in her ten years as a writer and graphic designer at *The South Bend Tribune*. She and her husband Kerry became the parents of triplets in August 2004.